How to Ride a Bike in a Dress

Published by Idea Creations Press
www.ideacreationspress.com

Library of Congress Control Number: 2014951077

ISBN-13: 978-0-9888107-7-8   ISBN-10: 0-9888107-7-8

Second Printing, 2015

Cover art by Rebekah JiWon Moon; Rebekah is a French and art student at Skyline High School in Salt Lake City, Utah. Rebekah offered to paint the cover as a service project for one of her Personal Progress goals. Layout and design by Susan Lofgren and Anna Oldroyd

Printed in the U.S.A.

DONNA PAULETTE YOUNG

How to Ride a Bike in a Dress

LIFELONG REFLECTIONS OF A SISTER MISSIONARY

Acknowledgements

"Merci mille fois" to my colleague and friend, Lisa Thornbrue, for finding time to edit and offer invaluable suggestions for my book between grading papers and inspiring future young writers in her high school classroom. Thank you also to my readers and friends, Cherie Sorensen, Patty Schmuhl, Lona and Tom Elmer, Dianna Dillingham, Mary Kaelin, Lora Johnston, Pam Turley, Roger and Mary England and Kathryn Jones for their encouragement, help and insightful suggestions. Thank you to Susan Lofgren and Anna Oldroyd, who graciously did the graphic design, and Rebekah JiWon Moon, who painted the beautiful art for the cover.

Thank you to all the wonderful sister missionaries, past and present, who gave me permission to use pictures of you and your bikes in this book.

Dedication

I would like to dedicate this book to Elder Burns K. Black and all the other missionaries who worked so valiantly with him in order to bring the message of the Restored Gospel of Jesus Christ to my parents in Philadelphia, Pennsylvania. We will love you forever!

A life-time of thank you's—and beyond—as well to my dear father and mother, Everett William Young and Bertha Brown Simon Young, who raised their children in the shining light of their faith. Thank you for teaching us about the Savior and His love through your life-long examples of unconditional love and devotion.

My dedication would be incomplete without mentioning all the wonderful missionaries and companions I had the privilege to serve with in the Brussels, Belgium Mission under the inspired leadership of President Virgil Parker, and his wife, Sister Jacquelyn Parker. The time I spent serving shoulder to shoulder with you continues to bless my life.

And finally, I most certainly must also include my three young friends, Grace, Eliza and Emma, who inspired the writing of this book.

What Others Are Saying

"With careful attention to detail and deep insight, Donna has captured the essence of a sister missionary experience. This book will not only resonate with returned missionaries, but will provide realistic and bright expectations for sisters preparing to leave." —Pam Turley, returned missionary, mother to nine missionaries

"I enjoyed reading this book very much and cannot wait for my daughter to read it before her mission. I could relate to almost every story in the book and felt as though I had just experienced my entire mission again. I am anxious to hear my daughter's thoughts about this book and know she will take some of these inspiring experiences with her on her mission." —Kim Peterson, returned missionary, Canada Montreal Mission, missionary mom

"This book is wonderful! It is written in such a beautifully descriptive manner that you can picture every story as it happens. You laugh, you feel the Spirit, and you are reminded of the transforming power of a mission. The book made me want to be a better person. The joy of the gospel will be replanted in your heart." —Patty Schmuhl, returned missionary, Brussels Belgium Mission

"Donna Young has created a delightful treasury of mission stories told with honesty, warmth and good humor. But le vrai tresor—the real treasure—lies in her having recognized and recorded the tender mercies of the Lord as He taught her with subtle, quiet power. One cannot read this book without marveling anew at the willingness of the Lord to love us and guide us each so personally and so poignantly." —Lisa Thornbrue, Editor

"As a missionary parent who has never personally served a mission, How to Ride a Bike in a Dress *gave me a new understanding of and appreciation for the missionary experience and the growth that takes place while these missionaries serve. This thoughtful account gives readers additional perspective and understanding of the missionary experience. I truly loved and appreciated this book!"*

—Amy Garff, Missionary Mom

"I was impressed with what a great vision this wonderful book offers to those who are looking at serving a mission. It also serves as a reminder to everyone, whether we have served a mission or not, of just how much the Lord's hand is a part of helping us through all of life's trials." —Doug Marriott, Marriott Development LC

"Wonderful and merveilleux! This will become an all-time classic for sister missionaries." —Chris Miasnik, mission comrade

" Reading How to Ride a Bike in a Dress *helped to eliminate my fears and answer the questions and concerns I had while I was preparing to serve a mission. It opened my eyes to the eternal blessings gained by serving a mission and helped me to know that the decision to serve was the right choice for me."*

—Sarah Simpson, Elementary Education major at University of Utah

"Upon reading Donna's book, I felt like putting on a dress, riding my bike up and down the streets of my neighborhood and singing 'Called to Serve' at the top of my lungs." —Don Horan, retired senior citizen

Notes about the book

When I left on my mission, the present-day MTC complex was in the process of being constructed. As a result, I actually started my mission at what was then called the Language Training Mission, or LTM. The LTM was housed on the lower campus of BYU in Knight-Mangum Hall. French missionaries studied in a building affectionately referred to as "B 30" (pronounced "bay" trente). For reasons of simplification for younger readers, I chose to use the term MTC when referring both to my own mission experience at the LTM as well as my post mission experience at the MTC.

I have drawn from my journal entries, letters and personal recollection in the retelling of these stories. Every effort was made to be accurate. Occasionally, when a few details were similar from two different experiences, they were combined to avoid unnecessary repetition.

In honor of my family's home teacher, Joseph Wood, who generously offered to help pay for my mission, a portion of the proceeds from the sale of this book will be donated to help support other missionaries who may be in need of financial assistance.

And oh, for all of you who may have also dropped out of eighth grade French, like me—or have never taken it at all—there is a glossary of the French terms that you will find throughout my stories at the end of the book.

You can contact the author at rideabikeinadress@gmail.com or visit her blog at
rideabikeinadress.wordpress.com

I'd love to hear from you!

Contents

PROLOGUE

Le Début

THE BEGINNING

The high school where I taught was buzzing with chatter. The new age guideline for missionaries had been revealed at the 2012 October General Conference by President Monson and everyone was talking about it, especially the seniors. For so many, their whole lives had changed in a matter of one weekend.

Not more than two days after that conference had concluded, I happened to catch sight of one of my usually shaggy-headed students walking down the hall sporting a new, close-cut, clipped-around-the-ears hair style. I almost didn't recognize him.

"Wow!" I remarked, "What happened? Did you run into a lawn mower or something?"

Without a second's hesitation, and with a grin that spread from ear to ear, he proudly announced, "I'm going on a mission!"

A few months later, I found myself enthusiastically engaged in an after-school conversation with three of my former students. All three girls had been student leaders in the school. They also happened to be sisters. Two of them were identical twins—not much more than a few months away from their nineteenth birthdays—while the other sister had turned twenty a few months previously. Several weeks before that, they had surprised me with a phone call one evening in which they had excitedly announced their simultaneous decisions to serve missions. Practically floating into my classroom and bubbling over with a hard-to-miss enthusiasm, they began to share the details of their individual calls. I couldn't help but notice that as obvious as their enthusiasm was, so was their nervousness. I felt my mind drift fondly back to a time— almost half a lifetime ago—when I had been in their place. I understood with perfect clarity their jumble of emotions as if it were yesterday. As the tender memories of my own mission filled my heart and I considered the marvelous and life-changing experiences that awaited these almost-to-be Sisters-sisters, I felt an unrestrained twinge of righteous envy flutter across my heart.

While serving a mission had not always been a part my life's plan, fortunately it had become one. The decision to serve a mission had had its quiet genesis one day while I was sitting on a hard bench in a dimly-lit locker room of a local college, deeply engrossed in a conversation.

I had just finished a practice session for the college softball team I played on when I happened to pass by the newest member of our team on my way out of the locker room. She had just returned home from a mission to Japan. In celebration of her return, she had invited our whole team to her home and generously treated us to a wonderful Japanese dinner the night before. It had been a wonderful, culturally enriching evening. I remember feeling intrigued by the great understanding and love for the Japanese people and culture that our host had demonstrated.

When I happened to spot her the next day in the locker room, I stopped to thank her again for such a delightful evening. An hour and a half later, after our "little chat" had concluded—a chat which had managed to evolve into an informal question-and-answer period about what a mission was like—I left that dingy, gray locker room feeling unusually uplifted and inspired. Although I didn't know it at the time, I would find out soon enough that a tiny seed had been planted in my heart that day—one that would continue to grow over the coming weeks and months until it eventually forced me to take notice of it.

At first, as if out of nowhere, the little thought would occasionally flash across the screen of my mind and tease me with the idea of serving a mission. Even though I had always had a strong testimony of the church and a great love for the Lord, I had nevertheless never considered a mission—and still wasn't considering one. I had definite plans for my life and was right in the middle of trying to make them happen. Besides that, the whole idea of serving a mission frankly terrified me; I just couldn't imagine myself doing what I knew missionaries were required to do. It felt in many ways so terribly out of my own comfort zone. As a result, when those mission thoughts started to quietly sneak into my head, I would quickly and resolutely dismiss them one by one by carefully going down the prepared list of reasons I had made in my mind as to why a mission just wasn't for me.

First, I would tell myself, there was the question of my studies that I would have to abandon right in the middle of the intensive program I was enrolled in. Next, there was my family's financial situation, which was a very real concern. And of course, there was my social life that I was trying desperately to nurse along. Initially, it was quite easy to find a myriad of reasons to dismiss the idea when thoughts of a serving a mission would slip into my mind during unguarded moments. The excuses I had come up with all seemed to be quite plausible, as well as worthy alternatives to serving a mission. For some time, they did a remarkable job of staving off the desire to seriously give the thought any further consideration. But that didn't last for long.

Over time the Spirit began to work on my heart. Ever so subtly the validity of my reasons for not serving a mission started to wither away and I soon realized that I could no longer ignore the incessant battle that had begun to rage in my head. It felt as though the "to go, or not to go" debate had so thoroughly hijacked every unconscious thought in my mind that it was practically impossible for me to think of anything else. Finally, when my last excuse had tumbled away and I was left exposed to my deliberating, bare inner self, I knew it was time to seriously ask the Lord what He wanted me to do with my life. One weekend, when I was out of school and had some time to carefully reflect on things, I decided to fast and pray for answers.

The answer to my prayer came as powerfully as any answer I had received up to that point in my life; I simply knew without a doubt that I was to serve a mission. With that answer, and my eventual call to serve, an almost overwhelming excitement—mingled with some nervousness—transformed my soul from head to toe with its electricity. It was the same mélange of sentiment I could see registered in the eyes and on the faces of the three sisters who sat before me in my classroom so many years after my own mission.

As I thought about what the future had in store for them, there was so much I wanted to tell them about a mission—so many stories I wanted to share. These stories—and the lessons derived from these stories—had directed and sometimes carried me through a lifetime of rich experiences. They were tender, soul-enlarging stories that had interwoven themselves around the very fibers of my heart and which had, in one way or another, impacted each and every single day of my life. I wondered where I could ever begin to tell my three young friends what a mission was like and what it would mean to them. I didn't even know where to start.

"I found out that I will be riding a bike on my mission!" the older sister readily volunteered, bringing my thoughts to an abrupt focus.

I felt a smile slowly rise in my heart as I shared with her that I too had ridden a bike on my mission. At that, the all-important, inevitable question was asked. It was the same question that I'm sure every sister missionary who has ever been assigned to labor in a mission from the seat of a bike has ever asked, since time immortal.

"So, how do you ride a bike in a dress?" questioned one of the twins with an absolutely perplexed expression on her face.

"Ah yes, that," I mused. Fond memories of a dear two-wheeled friend I had left so many years ago in a far off land washed over me. "It's much easier than you think," I continued, with what I am sure was a far-off look in my eyes, "Let me tell you how."

CHAPTER ONE

Le Vélo

The Bicycle

> *"In two years my life was changed forever and forever and forever. Everything I hold dear, everything I cherish in one way or another, I owe to the experience that converged from my childhood, my lovely parents, and my good home. Converged and passed into my soul on a mission. . . . Everything that has ever blessed me I owe to the gospel, collectively, broadly, and to my mission specifically"* (Elder Jeffery R. Holland, "The Miracle of a Mission," Brazil CTM, Oct. 28, 2000).

With each turn of the wheel I could feel the tiny drops of dirty rain as they flipped up from the rear tire of my bike and spattered across the back of my dress. I realized that any preparation I had made that morning to carefully style my hair and choose my outfit in anticipation of the first time I would be meeting the members of the branch, had been wasted effort. It wasn't really raining, just misting lightly, but ten minutes of biking in this kind of weather had been enough to make my hair stick to my back in long unruly clumps, and to send little streams of water dripping off the tip of my nose and rolling down my chin. Futilely, I blinked at the annoying drops that clung to my lashes in an attempt to clear my vision and try to locate my companion who was somewhere far ahead of me.

Although I had considered myself to be in pretty good shape when I'd left on my mission, as I had conditioned daily and played on sports teams for the past couple of years in college, I was still no match for the almost-one-year-out mission legs and lungs of my quickly disappearing companion. A companion who, though I pedaled as hard and fast as I could, somehow managed to remain one or two blocks ahead of me. Secretly I prayed—though somewhat guiltily—as I huffed and puffed up to each intersection, that my guardian angels would be so kind as to turn all the green lights red before I got to them. At least then I would have a respectable excuse to stop and catch my breath.

My failure to keep pace with my companion, coupled with the endless fatigue I was battling, had taken me somewhat by surprise: I hadn't expected to feel so overwhelmingly tired all the time. Certainly, I had been a little bleary-eyed right at first when I had entered the MTC—at least until I had gotten used to the early to bed, early to rise, study-all-day routine. But I really thought it would get a little better once I actually got out into the mission field. However, since arriving in France, my mind had been constantly numb with the ever-present effects of jet lag. It was something I had never before experienced, especially since my flight to France had been my maiden voyage in an airplane.

For practically the entire thirteen hour flight to France, I'd sat with my face glued to the window watching every fascinating cloud, mile, and eventually, every kilometer as it passed by. Not wanting to miss a single solitary thing as we hopped from cloud to cloud, and zipped progressively forward through time zone after time zone, I had stayed put at my little window to the world for the entire flight. Unfortunately, I'd discovered—a little too late—that the one important thing I had missed out on was any semblance of a night's sleep, as abbreviated as it might have been. To my surprise, almost as soon as the sun had dipped suddenly below the glowing horizon, leaving the plane cabin dark for a few, brief moments, that shining ball of light had popped right back up in the sky, signaling to everyone and to everything—except to my body and my fuzzy head—that it was the beginning of a new day.

As a result of my sleepless night, and the fact that I had been running on adrenaline and nerves for the past who-knows-how-long, I was past the point of exhaustion when the group of missionaries I had been traveling with finally arrived in Brussels, Belgium some twenty-four or so hours after having left the Provo MTC. It hadn't helped that the Mission Home staff chose to conduct our official Mission Home welcome by gathering us all together on a soft couch. A couch which in my half-hallucinating, sleepy mind, strangely resembled the comfortable mattress I was missing so much from a bed I had abandoned far too long ago. It was all I could do to keep myself from curling up into a little ball and nodding off into a dreamless, wonderful slumber.

Instead, valiantly I battled to prevent my droopy eyes from lazily rolling back into their sockets or worse, snapping permanently shut, all the while feeling as though I was nearly going cross-eyed in the effort. I felt absolutely starved for sleep and wondered if it were possible to die from fatigue. I was sure one could, and that I would.

I really thought my fatigue would ease up after I got a real night's sleep—not that any night on a mission could ever be considered "real sleep." It was a fact I discovered was especially true those first few nights in the field. Every night, as consistently as a dripping faucet, my eyes would pop open wider than I could ever remember them being open at the unearthly hour of 2 AM. Confused and totally disoriented, I would struggle to focus in the darkness, made even blacker by tightly shuttered windows, in an effort to make any sense out of all the shadowy, unfamiliar objects that surrounded me. As there was really nothing I could do at that wee hour of the morning that wouldn't disturb my companion slumbering peacefully in her bed, I simply passed the time staring at the ceiling. Either that or studying what I could make out in the small confines of my new home until I could fall back asleep again.

The apartment itself was not very big, but I soon discovered that it was more than adequate for the limited amount of time we would ever spend in it due to our jam-packed schedule. A tiny kitchen table, where I gulped down my first few breakfasts of better-than-American yogurt and then sat for daily companion study sessions, was not more than a few feet from the foot of my bed. A small kitchen veered off to the right of that; the kitchen came complete with a gas stove as well as an undersized fridge that probably didn't even reach my elbow—one reason, I learned, why so many French women still did their shopping for food and other such perishables on a daily basis.

Off to the right of my bed was a tiny catch-all table that separated my companion's twin bed from my own. There, perched like the merciless sentinel that it was, sat the enemy alarm clock, that mighty little guardian of time and ruthless thief of blissful slumber. Looking past the foot of my companion's bed, I could catch sight of the door at the end of the small hallway that led out of the apartment into the building corridor. Along a wall of that hall were found two doors, side by side, that divided what was typically a single

The Bicycle

room in an American home into two tiny rooms instead. One of the rooms was the bathroom, or "salle de bain," which was precisely that—a place to take a bath. There were no showers, unless of course you considered that hand-held, low-pressured squirty thing that you could let drizzle over your head as you sat in an odd-shaped tub, a "shower."

The other tiny room was the W.C., or water closet, so appropriately named by the English as after all, it was really only about the size of a coat closet. Figuring out what to pull and what to push to get the plumbing to work was an education in and of itself as nothing seemed to be standardized in the French plumbing system; each new faucet and lever had its own unique look and mode of operation. It was all so new and so confusing, especially when it became necessary to make a foggy-headed trek to that particular "petit coin" of the apartment during yet another sleepless night.

The dust from my sleepy arrival had barely settled when I was informed by my companion that it was time to face the challenge I had anticipated ever since I had first opened my pre-mission welcome letter. The few months previous, when I had sifted through the pages of that letter—which had been replete with such useful information as what to bring and what not to bring on a mission—my eyes had frozen when I got to one particular phrase near the end of the letter. Quite simply it stated, "You will need to purchase a bike once you arrive in the field."

For some reason, it had never dawned on me that I would be riding a bike on my mission. Even though I had a bike at home and occasionally even chose to ride it—for exercise—I couldn't imagine pedaling around town on one dressed as if I were ready to go to church. Generally when I had blown the dust off my bike and had taken it out for a spin, I had chosen to wear attire that I didn't mind getting at least a little bit sweaty in. This attire always included a good set of pant legs which would conveniently stay in place on pumping legs and not inflate like an uncontrollable parachute against a resisting breeze like a skirt would. Besides that, absolutely no girl older than ten years old would ever be caught dead riding a bike in a dress where I came from. It just wasn't done.

As I rubbed the sleep out of my eyes on that first bright and early morning, I reluctantly rolled myself out of bed. I was about to learn just exactly how I was going to ride a bike in a dress—for the next year and a half of my life.

Upon finishing our daily morning routine and planning session, my companion and I left our apartment to buy my new bike. Dutifully, I struggled to keep pace with my long-legged companion—who I quickly discovered never wasted a single, solitary second, ever—as she sped-walked her bike to the closest bike shop with me in tow. After I'd carefully picked out a brand-new light blue and silver, five speed bike, I pushed my new transportation out to the sidewalk and began the preliminary "riding a bike in a dress" adventure of my mission.

As my comp prepared to hop on her bike, I watched and meticulously mimicked her every move. I secured my bulging purse to my bike, precisely following my companion's example. I then hopped on my bike, making sure to carefully tuck between me and the seat of the bike—just as she had done—all and anything that might catch the wind and billow away. Finally mounted, tucked in and ready, I bravely took my first few missionary pedals out into the street. With that, I joined the throngs of girls, boys, teenagers, scarf-sporting middle-aged women, and elderly men in black berets and gray suits, who were blissfully biking alongside me as if they had done this their entire life. Which apparently they had.

At first it was difficult to determine who really had the right of way—something I'm still not sure even the French truly understand—as hordes of miniature toy-like cars seemed to be coming at me from every direction. But after a few close calls, it became more or less apparent that anything coming at you from a road on the right, whether a big, main street or simply a little, side "chemin," was supposed to have the right of way—"supposed to" being the key phrase. It took only a few blocks of precariously rolling down tiny canalled streets to learn that French drivers love to use their horns far more than they like to use their brakes. If that wasn't enough to send you scurrying out of their way, some would shake an angry fist out the window as they impatiently swerved around you.

Another important tidbit of knowledge I acquired quickly on that first bike outing was that the quaint cobblestone streets which gave this city its typical European ambiance—while a tourist's dream—were not a biker's friend. That is, unless you enjoyed the vibrating buzz that tickled your body right down to your white knuckles; knuckles which, in death-like fashion, clung to the handle bars in an effort to keep both you and the bike upright. It felt oddly like skiing moguls, something I really don't even enjoy doing

The Bicycle

on skis, where in split second increments you are forced to decide if you are going to go up or down with the uneven pavers or maneuver around them. That or pick yourself up from the ground. All this while trying to avoid cars that whizzed by you like teenagers on snow boards.

There was much to learn in the first few days of my mission and the lessons came fast and furious, some much faster than others. Like the lesson I learned when I took my eyes off a dirt-packed bike path in front of me for just the tiniest split second, which was exactly long enough to miss the fact that the path ahead veered suddenly to the left. Lying flat on my back in the weeds, staring groggily up into the sky, quickly convinced me that my companion, who herself was doubled over in an uncontrollable fit of laughter on the path I had just so unceremoniously left, was not my doting mother.

I felt things would have probably been better off had my comp just left me there in the weeds, and then come back for me at the end of the day, or even the next month. I'd felt as useless as a three-year-old as I'd tagged along on the few appointments we had already had since I had arrived. At that point, I'd been pretty much convinced that the language they had taught us in the MTC was not the same language they were speaking there in France.

After two months in the MTC—months which had felt like two years due to all that had been stuffed into those eight weeks—I had left the Missionary Training Center feeling ready to conquer and convert the "francophone" world. That is until I quickly discovered that I didn't understand the French, and it was painfully evident that they didn't understand me either.

As I pedaled to church in that light Sunday morning mist tired, soggy and discouraged, I could feel my spirit start to plummet until it matched the same shade of gray as the day—the effects of those first few short nights and the long, long days that followed had definitely taken their toll on me. Little by little, the excitement, the joy and the burning desire I'd felt for so many months in anticipation of serving a mission drizzled out of me and splashed into the puddles like the rain. I felt so terribly useless and so very alone in such a strange new land, surrounded by people I didn't know who couldn't understand much more than a word or two of what I attempted to say, and who knew little more about me than my last name. A wave of "mal du pays"—that empty missing of home and of things familiar— like I had never before known, washed over me and doused any enthusiasm that still remained. Longingly, I thought of my family and friends, who just days before had gathered to see me off at the airport. I could imagine them driving to the church house only a few blocks away, stepping out of their warm, comfortable, 'dry' cars, their clothing wrinkle-free and every hair still in place. I missed their hugs, their laughter, but most of all, I missed their presence.

Approaching the last leg of the journey, half-heartedly I stood up and pumped the pedals of my bike even harder so as to not lose sight of that tiny moving speck of a companion I had been so fixed on, for fear of becoming totally lost, forever. Out of breath, wet and now sweaty and muddy to boot, I felt my spiraling spirits take one last dip and hit rock bottom. As I blew away another annoying trickle of rain that had made its way to my mouth, I heard the question that I had been fighting to keep from forming in my mind during that entire wet and discouraging bike ride finally escape from my lips. "What on earth am I doing here?" I uttered to myself, and to anyone else who might have cared to listen.

About a block before we reached the church, my companion, having glanced back and finally noticing how far I had been trailing behind her, slowed down a bit and started making wide circles on her bike so that I could catch up and enter the building with her. Finding a slender tree, we locked our bikes to it and then made a beeline straight for the restroom where we could do a little damage control on our appearance before entering the meeting. As we passed through the doors that led to the small chapel area of the building, strains of a familiar hymn greeted my ears and caught my attention. After a brief welcome by one of the suit-and-tie, white-shirt-clad brethren seated on the stand, who I assumed to be the branch president, the pianist began a one-handed introduction for the opening song. Ever so subtly, something in my heart began to settle as I worked my way through the foreign pronunciation and tempo of a hymn I had sung since my childhood. I had always loved music and in particular the hymns. Many a night of my growing up years had been spent crowded around a piano, harmonizing with the other members of my family, as my mom played for us—sometimes for hours on end—the notes of those beautiful testaments of faith and devotion.

As we moved through each part of the Sacrament meeting, I was keenly aware that for the first time since I had arrived, I could understand most of what was going on simply by the familiarity of the context. A quiet, peaceful spirit prevailed throughout the meeting which filled my heart like the pres-

7

The Bicycle

ence of an old friend. Occasionally I would glance around at the congregation which, while tiny in comparison to the bursting-at-the seams ward I was used to at home, felt nevertheless comfortingly like glimpses of "chez moi." Here and there I caught the familiar sight of little clumps of "dressed in Sunday best" families, with mothers and fathers valiantly trying to keep the squirming children who sat between them reverent and at least somewhat attentive, just like they did back home. As I watched them worship, I felt surrounded by brothers and sisters in the gospel who, while I didn't know any of their names or recognize any of their faces, nevertheless had hearts I could feel and understand.

At the end of the meeting my companion and I moved out into the small foyer in order to greet some of the members who had come up to welcome and say "bonjour" to the new "soeur missionnaire." One by one they approached us and warmly introduced themselves to me, "les frères" shaking my hand, while "les soeurs" greeted me with the typical French "bise," or a kiss on either cheek—a greeting sometimes necessitating two, and sometimes even three, turnings of the cheek depending on which region of France the family originally hailed from. At first I felt a slight nervous awkwardness in this closer-than-I-was-used-to form of salutation as I tried to figure out which cheek I was supposed to turn first, and how I was supposed to know when I was done. The sincerity of their welcome, however, and the endearing title of "Soeur" followed by the brand new way I would hear my last name pronounced for the next year and a half, warmed my heart and brought a sunny ray of light into what had only hours before been a gray day.

As my companion and I slowly pedaled side by side back to our apartment that day, I reflected on the meeting and the members we had met with. I felt a gentle lifting of my spirit, as well as a peaceful, calming assurance that everything was going to be all right. What I couldn't have known, however, as I wheeled along on my shiny five-speed bike that Sunday afternoon, under much brighter skies than the day had started with, was just how much the next year and a half would change my life forever.

Post Script

While listening to an excerpt from an address that Elder Holland had delivered in 2007 to new mission presidents as they gathered to be trained at the Provo MTC, I found myself nodding in a silent agreement. "My mission means everything to me forty-seven years after the fact," he said with the sincerity one could always expect from Elder Holland. Then with his usual touch of gentle humor he quickly added, "There may have been one day in those forty-seven years that I have not thought of my mission; I'm just not sure what day that would have been."

I smiled to myself, knowing exactly what he meant. Although it had not been forty-seven years since my lonely bike ride to church as a brand-new missionary, it had already been several decades. There was no way I could have possibly known way back then how permanently those poignant, soul-stretching experiences that had filled those eighteen months of my mission would weave themselves around the daily threads of my existence, guiding my thoughts and actions for the rest of my life. But that is exactly as it has been.

"He that loseth his life for my sake shall find it." Matthew 10:39

The Bicycle

CHAPTER TWO

Le Don

The Gift

> *"Many of you who have gone to foreign lands have been given the gift to speak with tongues and to translate, or have the interpretation of tongues. 'And all these gifts come from God, for the benefit of the children of God' (D&C 46:26)" (Elder Robert D. Hales, "Gifts of the Spirit," Ensign, Feb. 2002).*

"Leur," my little dark-haired self-appointed tutor carefully pronounced, dropping his jaw and lingering purposely on the sound of that dreadful French "r."

"Leur," I painstakingly repeated.

"Non. Ce n'est pas comme ça," he corrected me again. Then resting his hands squarely on his small hips, like a relentless taskmaster, he waited for me to repeat the word after him.

That I needed help, and sooner rather than later, must have been painfully apparent to the angels over language acquisition as they seemed to be sending all the children of France to my rescue. The adults, upon failing to understand the nasal-like utterances I was attempting to make sound French, simply turned and looked questioningly at my companion and ask her to translate. The children, perhaps more empathetic to my situation, due to having emerged so recently from their own frustrating years of only being sporadically understood,

Left: Sister Young and Sister Dominault with Anne-Sophie

11

took it upon themselves to bring an obviously struggling foreigner up to speed.

"Leur," I repeated once more, thinking back on the last child-orchestrated language lesson I had received not more than a few days previously, only this time at the hands of four- year-old Anne-Sophie.

Earlier that week, in the home of Anne-Sophie's parents, after I'd made my minuscule contribution to the lesson my companion and I had prepared to teach, I'd then turned "la parole" back to my companion. She then proceeded to teach the rest of the lesson, while I took my "official role" on the couch next to Anne-Sophie as chief babysitter, in an attempt to somehow feel useful.

"Comment ça va?" I asked my new little charge who sat by my side. Or at least that's what I thought I asked her as two big brown eyes peered questioningly back up at me through large, oversized glasses. Almost as if on assignment, my soon-to-be instructor quietly slipped down from the couch, walked determinedly over to the bookshelf and retrieved a large picture book which she toted back to where I was sitting. As she took her place once more at my side, she plopped the book open, making sure that I could see it. Deliberately, she commenced turning the pages, pointing to objects one by one, waiting expectantly for me to correctly identify them. "Bateau," she patiently prompted me, pointing to the picture of a boat with one finger while pushing the glasses which had slipped to the end of her tiny nose up with another.

I knew right away that I was not going to get off the hook very easily in this little exercise as it had become evident that the French took great pride in their beautiful language starting at a very early age. "Bateau," she repeated once again, plainly not satisfied with my American-flavored French. "Bateau," I dutifully repeated, only this time being careful to leave out any trace of the nasal sound I had unconsciously been adding to every word just in case it was needed. And so it went, picture after picture—sometimes my efforts received a quick, satisfied "bien" and permission to go on to the next page, while others were soundly rejected with a scrunched-up nose and emphatic shake of a tiny head indicating that I had totally missed the mark and would need to try again. It was hard work achieving the final approval of my young teacher's critical ear before she resolutely turned the last page and closed the book on my language lesson for the day.

Not more than a few days following that first child-delivered language lesson by Anne-Sophie, I found myself once again fully embroiled, in "déja-vu" like fashion, in my next lesson with a particularly persistent dark-haired boy. In what appeared to be the ultimate trial of his patience, my new little tutor repeated once more the word that the entire success of my oral language experience seemed to depend. "Leur," he purposely over pronounced.

Deliberately, I placed my tongue behind my teeth, forced my jaw into a relaxed position and let the "leu" part of the word flow from my half-open mouth. Then, carefully closing down a part of my throat—further back then I had ever articulated a single sound—I forced a stream of air through in an effort to attach the final "r" that finished off the menacing word.

"Oui," my young teacher squealed in unrestrained delight, and to my pleasant surprise. "Oui, c'est ça!"

Elated, and admittedly somewhat taken back by my own victory, I carefully repeated it again, and then once again just to make sure.

"Oui, oui!" he gleefully exclaimed, clapping his tiny hands together as only a proud teacher could. But I had sensed, even before his enthusiastic affirmation had reached my ears, that at last, I had done it: I had conquered my nemesis, the French "r."

I don't remember much of the scenery that passed by as we biked to our other appointments for the rest of the day. All I can remember were the many signs along the way that somehow I had failed to notice before: stop signs, signs in windows, signs over stores, signs on billboards, advertisements on the sides of delivery trucks. I read each and every one of them out loud as I pedaled by them, pronouncing every word and every syllable I could catch sight of, letting that luscious French "r" roll effortlessly from the back of my throat, reveling each time in my newfound victory. It was a significant breakthrough I needed in what had been a long, hard, uphill road on my journey to learning the French language.

It had been made painfully clear, over the past few bumpy months of struggling to learn my mission language, that I had been clueless as to the direction my life would take when I had dropped out of my eighth grade French class after only two weeks. I had only signed up for the class in the first place because my older sister had signed up for French. Being the idolizing tag-along kid sister that I was, I always did everything that she did. Originally, it had sounded like such an exciting adventure, learning a secret language we could use to communicate right under the noses of our parents and especially under the noses of our other siblings. Night after night I would listen as my

The Gift

sister attempted to mimic basic conversations from the recordings she had borrowed from the school library. "Bonjour, Paul." "Bonjour Hélène." "Ça va?" "Oui, ça va, et toi?" Over and over she would play them, transporting the tiny bedroom we shared into a Parisian adventure.

The first day of 8th grade I could hardly wait to begin a French adventure of my own—that is until just two minutes into the very first class when I discovered in a panic that I was already completely and utterly lost. I hadn't counted on the fact that the teacher was actually going to be speaking French in class. Fear gripped my paralyzed heart as, after muttering a few unintelligible sounds over and over while pointing to herself, the teacher then started moving about the class pointing to us individually, like a sniper picking out unsuspecting victims. It was evident by the expectant look on her face that she actually wanted us to say something back to her. If at that point, there had been even the tiniest residue of sound that had somehow managed to lodge itself into my throat, it had completely evaporated into thin air by the time she had made her way around the room and finally stood in front of me. My brain froze as she pointed her loaded finger in my direction; my tongue, which lay helplessly paralyzed in my half-open, gaping mouth, couldn't have even uttered my own name in English, had she asked for it, which in retrospect, I think she had.

I suffered through the next two weeks until the school counselors took pity on me and released me from my torture by changing my class schedule. Heaving a sigh of relief, I resolutely determined that that little experience would be my last venture into the world of foreign language learning. And so it was—that is, until six years later when I excitedly opened the oversized envelope which contained the announcement that I would be serving in the Brussels Belgium mission and that I would be learning French.

After my call, I found new determination and began scouring through library after library in search of any "Learn Conversational French in Ten Days in your Sleep" recording I could find. Even so, I entered the MTC several months later knowing basically only what I had acquired by osmosis from those few French conversations that my sister had played over and over until she had lost fascination with learning French and had moved on to something else. Very quickly I learned that knowing how to say "Bonjour, je m'appelle Hélène" was only helpful if your name actually happened to be Helen, and that "Dis donc, où est la bibliothèque?" was absolutely useless unless, by chance, you were trying to find the library. The only other phrase I knew, and was sure would save me, at least for the first few weeks in the MTC, was "Je ne sais pas," which I thought I could conveniently use whenever I just didn't know the answer. Which I found out was always.

If I had thought that French had come at me rapid-fire during those two miserably long weeks of eighth grade French class, it had actually moved like frozen molasses in comparison to how fast MTC French now came at me at the rate of one of those French high-speed trains. What was covered in one day from a four-inch-thick, ten-pound "French For Missionaries" study guide felt like the entire junior high and high school curriculum being thrown at me in only eight hours of instruction. While my mind struggled to wrap itself around and retain one little aspect of the French language, the instructor would already be four or five concepts beyond that.

Every now and then, something would stick, but it was generally just enough to get me into trouble. Like the time I embarrassingly misinterpreted a question during our nightly retention period, which, in my opinion, was a grossly misnamed period of individual study time at the end of each day where we could theoretically work on "retaining" what we had learned in class that day. That would have been fine and dandy had there been something—anything—that had stayed long enough in my head to work on retaining it.

The particular evening in question, I had taken a break from another discouraging "retaining" experience in order to carefully pick my way through the long, crowded hall of white shirt-and-tie-clad nineteen-year-old Elders—with occasional sister missionaries mixed in between—in order to make my way back to the "W.C." at the end of the study hall. As I neared my destination, I passed by a small group of Elders who were studying together.

"Bonjour, Soeur," a friendly Elder in the district greeted me. "D'où venez-vous?" he quickly added, which I determined must be a question by the expectant look on his face.

"Où." Wildly I searched my mind, scrambling to come up with the meaning of what he had said, and vaguely remembered having gone over that in class. "Où"—that means "where!" It came to me out of the blue. As I lingered for a few painful seconds over the meaning of "venez," suddenly the image of moving from one place to another came to my mind.

"Where are you going?" my mind pieced together. "He's asking me where I'm going!" Somewhat embarrassed, I fumbled to give him an answer while still maintaining a small sense of privacy. As nothing came to my mind except for the few French words which happened to tell him precisely where I was

The Gift

going, I blurted out a little awkwardly, "les toilettes." Suddenly, to my bewilderment, the entire group of Elders erupted in uncontrollable laughter.

The blood rushed to my cheeks faster than I knew that blood could travel through veins. I managed to force a weak smile after which I sheepishly continued on my way to my desired destination, wondering all the while what in heaven's name I had just said that was so terribly funny. I found out soon enough.

Not more than a few seconds after returning back to the safety of my study table, following a careful detour that purposely avoided a second encounter with that same group of Elders, I discovered to my dismay the source of their amusement. A furious flip though that day's notes blatantly revealed the reason for their seemingly insensitive laughter. There, scrawled boldly in my own handwriting across the top of a page of my notebook I saw it: "D'où venez-vous." The explanation, which was there in the column—exactly where I had written it—stared back at me: "This literally means 'from where come you?' or 'where are you from?'" I had even underlined it. Twice. A lot of good that had done me!

At that moment, when I realized that I had basically just informed an entire district of Elders that my hometown was "les toilettes," I wished somehow the study hall floors would just open up and swallow me. I propped up my French grammar book and hid behind it for the rest of that evening, thankful for the first time that my book was so enormously large.

Through the next few days of language study which felt, at times, like a time warp in reverse, I gained a greater appreciation for just how very long eternity could feel—for the suffering at least—and how frustrating the tower of Babel incident must have been for our ancient ancestors; it was difficult to feel so continually and so completely confounded. I could feel a permanent furrow forming in my brow as I strained hour after hour to concentrate on the nonsensical sounds I was being spoon fed, and then attempted to remember them long enough to repeat them back—never mind trying to actually understand what any of those sounds meant. When we did learn new vocabulary, it didn't help that the spelling didn't look anything like the way the words were pronounced. This fact just about made me crazy one class period when my MTC teacher casually crossed out the final three, perfectly good letters in the conjugation "viennent," informing us that they were all silent—something I was finding out was the case for at least half the letters of the alphabet if they had the misfortune of coming at the end of a French word.

"Why, why, why do they put those letters there if they aren't going to say them?" The perfectly logical question escaped my tongue before I could pull it back, which caused the instructor to spin his head around and stare at me in bewildered astonishment and then begin an impromptu lecture on the irregularities of our own sometimes illogical language. I wasn't trying to be impertinent; it was simply more than my poor befuddled mind could tolerate at that point in my struggling language learning experience. It seemed so terribly unfair to have to cram into my head—which was already full to bursting—all those unused letters, if they weren't even needed! It was as if the French were in such a great hurry to say what they wanted to say that they couldn't even make it through a whole word before hurrying on to the next. To me, it made absolutely no sense.

One particularly frustrating evening during retention period, while flipping back through the pages of notes I had taken on the new vocabulary and grammar principles that had been presented in class that day, I felt as though I had forgotten just about everything we had covered. I knew I was already scraping along at the bottom of the class and worried that I would just keep falling further and further behind until one day it would be impossible to catch up. I feared never getting past the point of communicating in only one or two generally mispronounced words and phrases, which were only understood—when they were—with the help of vigorously injected charades and the fact that I could point at objects around me. I couldn't imagine ever being able to string enough of these foreign sounds together to ever communicate what I really wanted to say, let alone to be an effective missionary. Even though I could rationally reason that thousands upon thousands of missionaries before me had successfully learned their mission language—at least well enough to impressively bear their testimony at the end of their homecoming speech—I was finding it harder and harder to push away the nagging fear that kept sneaking into my mind that maybe, just maybe, I would be the one missionary who would never learn the language. It seemed that even though I was rowing with all my might, and giving everything I possibly had to learn this language, my little boat was starting to take on water and threatening to sink into the deep, dark abyss of discouragement and despair.

That evening, feeling so terribly unsure and afraid, I placed my head in my hands and in quiet desperation uttered what was perhaps the most simple, yet sincere and heartfelt prayer I had ever prayed: "Help me!" I desperately pled as I laid my head down on my arms in an act of final submission.

The Gift

I didn't spend more than a few minutes in that position before I slowly gathered myself together, lifted my head and started looking back through my notes once more. This time, miraculously and to my bewilderment, everything made perfect sense. It was as if a missing puzzle piece had somehow snapped into place, giving me a complete view of what that corner of the picture was supposed to look like. It was an odd sensation staring at those same pages which, only minutes ago, had seemed so meaningless and confusing to me; only now as I turned each page, each new concept somehow seemed to fit together in a logical, comprehensible manner. What was even more astonishing than that was that I could tell it was staying in my head. Still, not totally convinced of what was happening, I opened my book up and started skimming through page after page of earlier chapters that had previously eluded me. This time through, however, everything was perfectly clear. I understood, and more importantly remembered, everything we had covered in class.

I knew that something very significant had happened that night. While in reality, it was just a tiny part of the language that had been opened up to me—a few conjugations and several simple sentence structures here and there—nevertheless, the understanding and reassurance I had gained in those few moments were huge. In that brief moment, I had learned, in a way I would never forget, that if I could remember to become humble, submissive and teachable, and ask for help from the greatest Teacher of all, He could open up my mind and teach me absolutely anything, even French. It was an understanding that rooted itself deeply into my heart and which I found would not only help and guide me throughout the duration of my mission, but would guide, direct and teach me anything I wanted to know throughout the rest of my life.

At that point, even though I understood there would still be many difficult days ahead which most certainly would require a lot of hard work and patience on my part, I was comforted with the quiet surety that the language would eventually come, when it was needed, and it would come as a gift from heaven.

I would also find out, once out in the mission field, that the heavens would send me other special help along the way—help that would come in many different shapes and sizes, sometimes at the hands of, or more precisely, through the mouths of even His tiniest angels.

Post Script

"Viennent" I wrote on the board at the front of the class, resolutely crossing out the final three letters of the third person plural conjugation of the verb "venir." "The last three letters are silent," I carefully explained to my class of high school French students, trying my best to ease the frustration I could see mounting in their furrowed brows at the thought of so many wasted letters in a French word.

It was a lesson I'd taught at least a hundred times over the many years I'd enjoyed in my career as a secondary French teacher in the public education system. It was a lesson that would forever remind me of a loving Heavenly Father and of His tender gifts sent from heaven to a young and struggling sister missionary—gifts for which I will be eternally grateful.

"Be thou humble; and the Lord thy God shall lead thee by the hand, and give thee answers to thy prayers" Doctrine and Covenants 112:10.

Sister Sanders
Nagoya Japan Mission, 1999

The Gift

CHAPTER THREE

Le Voyage

The Journey

> *"Often the deep valleys of our present will be understood only by look-ing back on them from the mountains of our future experience. Often we can't see the Lord's hand in our lives until long after trials have passed. Often the most difficult times of our lives are essential build-ing blocks that form the foundation of our character and pave the way to future opportunity, understanding, and happiness"* (Elder Dieter F. Uchtdorf, *"Continue in Patience,"* Ensign, *April 2010*).

The view from the top was magical. Like nothing I had ever experienced. The walls of the imposing castle loomed behind me as the seemingly end-less valley spread out below me as far as the eye could see. I felt as though I were a character in a child's book of fairytales living a dream taken straight from its pages. It had been an unforgettable day visiting the castle, as I'd stepped back through the annals of time and had aimlessly wandered through the many lavishly decorated rooms, climbing the time-worn stone stairs and ramparts that still protected the memory of a time and a people long since departed.

I had been more than a little excited when I had first learned that our dis-trict would be visiting a famous castle in the region on what was to be a district-wide P-day. Having embarked on my mission experience fully anticipating that I would be spending each and every waking hour of the next year and a half either knocking on doors and/or teaching lessons, I was pleasantly surprised to

learn that occasionally there would be official time set aside from our missionary duties to relax and enjoy some of the beautiful cultural and historical sites in the country in which we served. The thought of a small break from the normal routine, coupled with the possibility of visiting a real live castle—the things that dreams were made of—was exhilarating to say the least.

The day started bright and early as we assembled at the local "gare" to begin our long anticipated journey to the castle. With our missionary tags pinned prominently to our P-day attire, complete with ear-to-ear smiles, we carefully wheeled our bikes through the crowded foyers of the train station. After locating the "petite salle" where our bikes were checked on to the train, we piled into the train ourselves and settled down in our seats. Momentarily, the train moved out of the station and the rhythmic clicking of the wheels against the steel tracks began to pull us further and further away from the city limits and deeper into the heart of "la campagne." I sank back into my seat, mesmerized by the beautiful verdant fields and rolling hills of the French countryside that flew by my window. Occasionally I caught sight of small red-roofed villages tucked away up against the hills, each one proudly encircling a spiral topped church—the jewel of each little town.

It wasn't a lengthy train ride, but long enough to whisk us far away from anything that even remotely resembled a large city. Upon arriving at the small town that was to serve as our launching point, we gathered together in the minuscule train station foyer and then wheeled our bikes out into the street to commence what would essentially amount to our very own mini twenty kilometer "Tour de France."

The initial leg of the trip wound us through little country roads, where occasionally we would catch sight of traditional farmers out in their fields, some still nostalgically choosing to plow their fields behind large teams of horses instead of availing themselves of the convenience of modern machinery. I felt as though I had stepped back in time as we pedaled through splendid tiny villages made up of quaint flower-box-accented stone buildings—some easily as old as the United States—all woven together into tight little communities by the narrow cobblestoned paths that wound through them. Gracefully arching stone entrances half exposed the concealed secrets at the heart of each village, playfully teasing a curious visitor to enter and explore.

Taking a brief pause inside one of these small villages, the one which marked the approximate midway point to our destination, we dismounted our bikes and propped them up against the stony circumference of a large fountain situated in the middle of a tiny cobblestone square. Cupping our hands, we drank deeply from the cool spring water that issued forth freely from several spouts jutting out from the tall central base of the fountain. As the cool water trickled down my thirsty throat, I wondered just how many a weary traveler had done exactly the same thing over the centuries that this fountain had graced this beautiful little village.

Just before mounting our bikes and continuing on with the rest of the journey, one of the Elders excitedly pointed off into the distance, exclaiming, "That's where we are going. The castle is on top of that mountain."

Following the direction of his pointing finger, my eyes squinted into the horizon until I caught sight of a triangular-shaped hill that rose up like a natural pyramid some four or five miles in the distance. Even from that distance I could tell that its slopes were steep—steeper than any mountain I had ever ascended without the assistance of something with a motor or an engine attached—yet I had the benefit of neither. It was just me and "mon vélo," embarking on what I would soon find out would be the climb of my life.

After a few deceivingly easy kilometers over the relatively flat terrain that separated us from the ascending part of our journey, our little group arrived at the base of the looming hill—which had become progressively larger and more foreboding the nearer we approached. After a short, courage-gathering "arrêt" and pep talk at the bottom, our district leader resolutely hopped on his bike, shouted an encouraging "bonne chance" over his shoulder and turned to attack the mountain.

"That's where we are going.
The castle is on top of that
mountain."

I shoved off a few pedals behind my companion and set my wheels on the upward path. I hadn't gone too far before it felt as though someone had set the emergency brakes on the wheels of my bike. As I battled to overcome the steadily increasing resistance of my efforts to advance, I understood with perfect clarity why the builders of the castle had chosen a position on the top of such a high hill; the gravity of its steep slopes ferociously fought against me as if I had been an entire invading army. I only achieved a few turns in the road before my calves and thighs began to burn and my pumping lungs commenced to scream in my ears.

Valiantly, I rose to a standing position and pumped even harder against the pedals in an effort to keep from stopping dead still in my tracks, or worse, rolling backwards and relinquishing precious parcels of conquered turf. Centimeter by centimeter I continued on as the hard-fought-for terrain rolled stubbornly past the laboring rubber of my tires. Silently I debated—as I gasped for what I felt could very well be my last breath—as to whether it would be worse to stop and walk my bike for a brief moment, at the risk of appearing to be a wimp, or to simply continue on and expire while still in the saddle.

I almost broke out into the Hallelujah Chorus—and would have had there been even the tiniest milliliter of oxygen left in my lungs—when I caught sight of my companion just a short distance ahead come to a full stop and jump off her bike to walk it up the steep incline. Forcing myself to push through a few more hard pumps, I brought myself up to what I esteemed to be a more respectable few feet behind her, then hopped off my bike as well. Huffing and puffing, my companion and I pushed our bikes forward, stopping every few meters to take in the scenery before us and to offer each other encouraging words of support. The minuscule reprise from the heat of the battle was, however, far too short to sufficiently provide a full recovery when—to my utter dismay—my companion resolutely jumped back onto her bike to continue on with the fight. Dutifully, I climbed back onto my own bike and recommenced the painful pumping and perspiring routine.

For the next physically tortuous hour and a half, the same scenario repeated itself over and over again as I slowly crept up the mountain. The sheer excitement of seeing the castle that had once propelled me to even consider such an arduous journey, had long disappeared, and my entire focus had shifted to simply enduring and surviving the battle at hand. Occasionally, the steep terrain would temporarily flatten out, offering a brief pause in the climb where I could look around and catch sight of the beautiful forest that surrounded me and remember, for a brief moment, the reason for the journey. But then, not more than a few meters up the hill, the gut-wrenching battle to just keep ascending began once again.

Finally, after what felt to be forever, I joyfully caught sight of the crest of the hill. I rounded the final curve and beheld the immense outer wall of the castle rising up before me. A wave of gratitude and relief rushed through my weary body as I realized the hard-fought battle was finally over, and that I had made it to the top. As I joined the others where they had propped their bikes against a small retaining wall in order to peer out into the endless horizon, an inexplicable feeling of accomplishment rushed through my body. I had conquered the mountain—and myself—pedal by pedal.

Somehow I sensed that the lessons derived from this "petite victoire" would take me to the tops of many more beautiful mountains and hills in my journey through my mission and through the years to follow. I felt strengthened in knowing that if, in those sometimes difficult climbs, I could simply remember to continue pumping and moving ever forward and upward, I would eventually reach a glorious—and sometimes even magical—summit.

At the top of Haut-Koenigsbourg Castle, Orschwiller, France

The Journey

Post Script

The straining whine of the tour bus as it struggled to slip into a lower gear was practically lost in the excited din made by the escalating voices of the junior high and high school-aged students that filled its seats. It had been decades since my own personal battle as a missionary, astride a blue and silver five-speed bike, to win this mountain we now climbed in comfort. With a quiet sense of gratitude, I looked out the window of the bus as the steep terrain of the windy road slowly slipped by my front row seat.

It was a dream come true to be able to share such a fairytale-like experience with the students I taught, and with the few members of my family who had been able to accompany me on this return trip to Europe. I wished I could also share how I owned that mountain as well as the valuable lessons it

We lined up our bikes and took a picture of the group before we started back down the hill. Going up the mountain had taken an hour and a half. Going down took about 15 minutes. I could smell my brakes burning all the way down, and several times felt very lucky that I hadn't gone off the edge on some of the sharp bends.

had taught me as a young missionary–metaphorical lessons in endurance that had pulled me through some of the more difficult periods of my mission and of my life.

As my anxious group of travelers noisily piled out of the idling bus and clamored over to the small retaining wall opposite the base of the looming castle to catch their first glimpse, I stood back and watched with the anticipation of a parent waiting for children to open their first Christmas package.

"Isn't it beautiful up here?" I heard one of my students exclaim above the excited clatter that issued forth from my small group as they peered out over the large expanse of valley that spread before them.

"Indeed it is," I quietly concurred as I reflected back on my own personal journey up the mountain and all it had taught me. "It is magical. Simply magical."

"But he knoweth the way I take; when he hath tried me, I shall come forth as gold. My foot hath held his steps, his way I have kept, and not declined"
Job 23:10.

The Journey

Sister Derksen
Japan Kobe Mission
2014

CHAPTER FOUR

La Connaissance

Knowledge

> *"Our missionaries meet people who have studied philosophy and metaphysics, world history, and languages, science and the arts. They meet people who are better educated than they are. . . . We cannot compete with the world on its terms. If we have the Spirit of the Lord to guide us, we can teach any person, no matter how well educated, anyplace in the world. The Lord knows more than any of us, and if we are His servants, acting under His Spirit, He can deliver His message of salvation to each and every soul"* (Elder Dallin H. Oaks, "Teaching and Learning by the Spirit," Liahona, *May 1999*).

A little knowledge can be a dangerous thing. Not only for a scholar scoffing at truth, but also, I discovered, for a well-intentioned sister missionary. I learned this important gem of truth in a never-to-be-forgotten manner during the early months of my mission, when my companion and I had the unusual opportunity of teaching a priest of another religion about our faith during several weekly rendezvous.

At one such meeting, we had prepared to show him filmstrips about scholarly evidence regarding the Book of Mormon. My job that evening was simple: I was to run the projector while my companion answered questions about the filmstrip. As it turned out, it wasn't quite so simple as that—a fact which I soon discovered when I plugged the projector in and nothing happened. After checking a few switches, with no success, I pulled the plug out

and set about to examine it to see if I could detect any problems. I was proud of myself when I discovered a loose wire dangling from the plug which I immediately determined to be the source of the problem. Confident that I knew at least a little about how electricity worked, I resourcefully pulled a fingernail file out of my bulging purse and set about to carefully re-attach the suspect wire to one of the screws in the plug. The repair accomplished, I silently congratulated myself on a job well done and I reached out to once again push the "now-fixed" plug back into the outlet. My surprise couldn't have been more complete when instead of the quiet hum of a projector starting up, I was instead sent reeling back by the sound of a loud "pop" and the sight of a puff of thick black smoke.

Instantaneously, the entire rectory was plunged into darkness except for a small stream of sunlight that trickled through a window into the shadowy library where we—just minutes before—had been so comfortably seated ready to begin our presentation. In the ensuing seconds, the priest, who had generally maintained a cordial "politesse" throughout our previous visits, turned and shot an icy, disbelieving glare in my direction. If looks could kill, it seemed the priest was seriously tempted to infringe upon the sixth commandment.

"Je m'excuse," I timidly offered, barely raising my head enough to catch a peek of him as he hurriedly rose from his chair and exited the room into the darkened exterior. Seemingly from out of nowhere, and within only a matter of minutes, the darkness was filled with the confused voices of numerous frantic nuns who, like squirrels whose nest had just been disturbed, were madly scurrying up and down the darkened corridors of the rectory in search of a solution for the blackness that had descended upon them.

Guiltily, I returned my attention to the site of the crime and discovered—to my horror—that a large black smudge had darkened the wall immediately encircling the now useless socket. Helplessly, I glanced at my companion who offered absolutely no solace from her corner as she sat shaking her head and rolling her eyes in a look of incredulity.

Suddenly, the whole scene—the blackened wall, the nuns running up and down the hall, the priest running behind them with his hands thrown frantically up in the air—struck me as being hilariously funny. Feeling a giggle start to rise in my throat, I clamped my lips closed and held my breath in an effort to divert my mind and attempt to suppress the threatening giggle from progressing any further up my throat—almost strangling myself in the process. But to no avail.

It was a vicious circle—the more I consciously tried not to think of the scene before me, the funnier it seemed and the more ferocious the battle became to try and stifle the urge to laugh. It was a battle I could tell I was quickly losing as exploding bursts of laughter started to force their way through my lungs like errant children trying to escape from school. My shoulders began to quiver and shake like an idling Model T Ford. I bore down and fought futilely to gain control. Muffled snickers emanating from where my companion was seated caught my attention and verified that she was fighting the same battle, only in her corner.

Having been raised in a household of girls, and knowing only too well how dangerous these giggling attacks could get once unleashed—and how long they could sometimes last—I diligently kept my head staring straight down at the floor, purposely avoiding even the slightest peek at my companion. I knew that such a seemingly lighthearted reaction to a mini-crisis might not be very kindly received by the priest and his rectory full of frantic nuns. Hoping that the escalating search for the fuse box would buy my companion and me the necessary time we needed to regain our composure, we individually fought our giggling battles in our respective corners, carefully avoiding any eye contact.

Though our discussions with the priest had been a regular part of my missionary experience ever since I had arrived in my first city, the details of just how he had come in contact with the sister missionaries and then agreed to receive their weekly visits was still a bit of a mystery to me. All I knew was that I had arrived on my mission right smack "en plein milieu" of the whole experience, which had initially proven to be the source of not a small amount of anxiety for me as I considered the prospect of teaching a priest as a newbie missionary. Week after week I watched and marveled at how boldly my companion presented each concept, each principle of the gospel. I couldn't detect even so much as a flinch or the slightest hesitation during such potentially sensitive subjects as infant baptism and eternal marriage. Humbly, I watched and learned as I witnessed the Holy Spirit guide and enlighten my companion lesson after lesson.

At first, the priest, who sat politely through each discussion, seemed interested enough and occasionally asked for clarification from time to time. Though I was never certain if he was just feeding his intellectual curiosity about our church or if he really wanted to know more for spiritual reasons, one thing was sure—the Spirit had been there quietly guiding what was

Knowledge

being taught. I was almost certain that he at times had felt it, as I had observed him quietly reflecting about something that had been said, even if only momentarily.

I noticed a distinct change in his demeanor, however, when our meetings with him started to move from merely teaching him to asking him to act. This was particularly true after he had been asked to pray if what he had been taught about the Book of Mormon was true.

"I can't do that," he flatly replied, insisting instead that he wanted to see some physical proof of the origin of the Book of Mormon.

He would counter our challenge to pray by insisting that the Bible was all he needed—that there was nothing in the Book of Mormon that couldn't be found in the Bible.

Attempt after attempt was made to point out principles that we had shared with him which were either uniquely taught or greatly clarified in the Book of Mormon but that were not found in the Bible. Each time he would respond with the frustratingly circular reasoning that he could not believe such a thing because it was not found in the Bible.

After one particularly spirit-filled lesson about the eternal nature of families, the priest responded to our invitation to pray to know if what we taught was true by inquiring, "So what real difference would it make for me to know that?"

In the minutes that ensued, and in the same quietly confident manner that had characterized each and every lesson that had been taught, my companion explained to the listening priest that our purpose as missionaries was to teach these truths and then to invite those who received a testimony as to their truthfulness—through the Holy Spirit—to be baptized into "L'Église de Jésus Christ des Saints des Derniers Jours."

There was a loaded pause for a brief moment before the priest responded. "So what you're telling me is that if I believed what you are teaching me is true then I would basically be out of a job."

"Essentially, yes," my companion confirmed without even so much as batting an eye.

The priest ended our appointment that evening by once again countering our invitation to pray with his customary, "I need to see some physical proof of the Book of Mormon,"

Thinking that we could at least show him a few of the filmstrips we had in our possession that highlighted discoveries made in Central and South America which were in harmony with various aspects of the Book of Mormon, we decided to bring a projector we had borrowed from the church when we met with him for our next appointment. It had seemed like such a good idea in light of his seemingly insatiable appetite for academic proof. That is until I had plunged his rectory into sudden darkness by my insufficient knowledge of how French plugs work.

After about ten minutes of scrambling confusion, the lights finally flicked back on and the priest returned to his chair in the library. With what amounted to miraculous constraint, my companion and I ended up teaching—"sans" projector—a completely different discussion than the one that we had originally planned with not so much as one solitary giggle escaping between us. We left the priest that day promising to bring back the filmstrips—and a different projector—for our next visit.

At the conclusion of our successful showing of the filmstrips on our next visit, and a short discussion which followed, the mood of the priest was noticeably more reticent and not nearly so welcoming or accommodating as he had been on previous occasions.

"That filmstrip told me absolutely nothing," the priest flatly remarked when we asked him about his feelings concerning the Book of Mormon. When asked if he had prayed to know if what we had challenged him to read in the Book of Mormon was true, he immediately responded, "Non."

He then paused a brief moment before the tone of his voice noticeably changed. Obviously agitated, he began to scold us as if we were two young naughty children who had been caught with our hands in the cookie jar.

"Who do you think you are trying to teach educated people like me about something you know very little about?" he condescendingly questioned. "I have dedicated my life to the study of the Bible and of ancient languages to arrive at what I know," he pronounced with a detectable air of self-importance. Then, gaining steam, he continued on with his lecture, "You are young, naive girls who are going around trying to deceive uneducated people with facts that aren't true so that you can get them to follow you," he finally concluded, somewhat red-faced from his spontaneous tirade. After a brief moment to gather her thoughts, my companion began to calmly and carefully reply to his reprimand, "You are right. We are not scholars like you are in ancient languages, or in theology." Then with an unmistakable power sustained by the Spirit which was so very present, she continued un-apologetically, "While there are many scholars in our church who are very educated in such things, and who could have been

nowledge

sent out to teach you instead of us, the Lord has sent us. We have not been sent here to try and convince you with our words, only to invite you to examine truths we have shared with you which can only be received through the Spirit. Man can teach us anything—truth or lies—while God will never deceive us. Through the Holy Spirit, He can and will teach us, any of us, what is truth, if we but ask."

The previous tension having dissipated, we once again asked him if he would be willing to pray about what we had shared with him. Finally assessing that he remained firm in his resolve not to accept our invitation to pray—and that his interest would now be purely academic—my companion quietly informed him that while we had appreciated the opportunity to meet with him, we would no longer be able to continue our visits. Suddenly, he looked dumbfounded, as if we couldn't possibly be serious about not coming back.

We then both bore our testimonies to him as to the truthfulness of those things that we had shared with him. As I bore mine, I experienced a powerful witness that the Spirit was directing my thoughts as well as a gentle assurance that I would never again have to be afraid of teaching the gospel of Jesus Christ to anyone—no matter their title or position—as long as the Spirit was there to guide my words and to fill my mouth.

As we rose to leave and I turned towards the door, my eye caught sight of the small trace of the soot-smudged spot which was still there on the wall, having somehow been missed in the initial clean up. I felt a sense of sincere regret tug at my heart as I realized with clarity how just a bit of academic knowledge had kept this little rectory from finding even more truth and light.

Post Script

A small path wound itself through dense jungle foliage as our small group of tourists followed the guide to the final set of ruins that my friend and I had planned to visit on our trip. This trip had been the furthest venture south of the border of the United States that I had ever taken and was one that I had wanted to take for quite some time. I had been intrigued by the many things I had learned over the years about various proposed sites for Book of Mormon events in Central and South America. I had looked forward with enthusiasm to the time that I could experience them myself.

A few days earlier at the beginning of our trip, I had listened with great interest as our guide introduced us to our very first set of ruins. It was evident that this guide, who was a local to the region, had a great deal of reverence for the land where these ruins were located. He informed us that the magnificent structures before us, once completely hidden beneath the layers of earth and lush trees and foliage that had covered them, had served as his childhood playground. When he was in his late teens and the ruins were uncovered by excavators, he was astounded to discover what those hills had been hiding beneath his feet for all those years—treasures of a people and of a time that had long since disappeared from view.

As I listened to the stories he told and to the theories he shared about the people who had lived there, who had thrived there by the thousands and then somehow vanished, I sensed a familiar stirring within me. I felt as though I were looking at a place and hearing stories about a people that I had been reading about my entire life. I could imagine some of the great battles and events that had taken place on this

Knowledge

very soil as well as the names of people and prophets who had written about such a time and place.

I felt that same familiarity as we tagged along with the next little group of tourists visiting our final set of ruins. It had required an hour boat ride up a winding crocodile-laden river before we had arrived deep in the heart of an imposing rain forest where the ruins were located. Thick vegetation surrounded us on every side as we made our way along the dirt path that twisted itself through the shadowy jungle. Rounding a curve in the path we were led by our guide to a large sunlit opening in the undergrowth which revealed a massive stone structure that the guide referred to as a possible temple for the people who had populated the area.

For nearly an hour we were led from one impressive structure to another. Throughout our visit, as the guide explained characteristics of the ruins and of the people who had built them, a member of our group kept pointing out similarities he detected between what he was seeing and hearing with things he knew about the people and world of the Bible.

"These look a lot like the step pyramids in Egypt," this tourist remarked as we gazed upon one of the magnificent structures before us. Then thoughtfully he questioned. "How did the inhabitants of this land learn to make the same kinds of structures that the Egyptians had made?"

His observations and comparisons to the Old World continued as we finished our visit to the imposing ruins that the jungle had kept so carefully hidden. Purposely, I slowed my step. I was walking beside him as we finished our tour.

"Those are interesting observations you made," I told him as we walked and talked about what we had seen.

Openly I shared with my new friend that these ruins had

an important significance to me and to the members of my faith. I then suggested that he might be interested in reading an important book that talked about the ancient inhabitants who had lived in this part of the world, who had built these structures and where it is that they came from.

Then thinking back on a time very long ago—of faulty projector plugs and of frantic nuns—I added with confidence fueled by the Spirit, "I believe that this important book of which I speak, The Book of Mormon, may be able to shed a great deal of light on your questions."

"That which is of God is light; and he that receiveth light, and continueth in God, receiveth more light; and that light groweth brighter and brighter until the perfect day" Doctrine and Covenants 50:24.

Sister Lund, Dunkirk, France, 1976 on a P-day with a week's worth of groceries and laundry loaded on her bike.

Knowledge

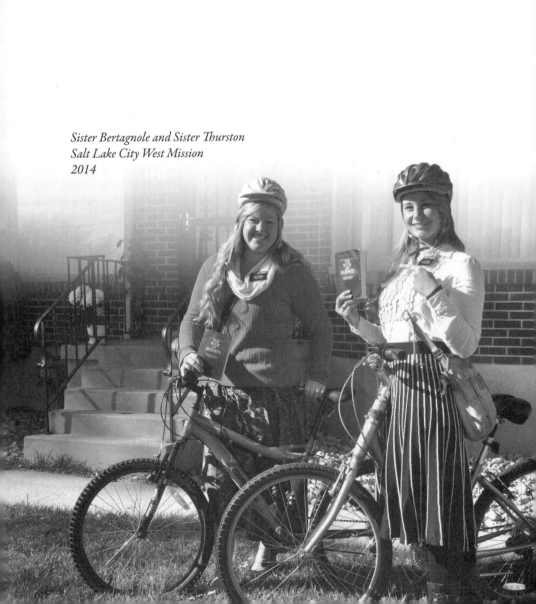

Sister Bertagnole and Sister Thurston
Salt Lake City West Mission
2014

CHAPTER FIVE

La Réponse

The Answer

> *"The Book of Mormon offers a remarkable promise to those seeking knowledge of the truth. . . . [Moroni. 10:3–5] In addition to the great promise in these verses which helps those who are investigating the gospel to gain a testimony of the Book of Mormon, the process Moroni teaches here can be used in confirming all truth. This is a process we can go through every time we wish to have eternal truth confirmed"* (Elder Gene R. Cook, "Moroni's Promise," Ensign, *April 1994*).

knew immediately from the raised eyebrows of my companion and the hurried glance she shot at me that I had said something wrong. Although I was still pretty new when it came to presenting this entire section of the discussion to our investigators—the part about Joseph Smith's first vision and of his subsequent visits from the angel Moroni before receiving the gold plates—I had generally been able to make it all the way to the end without my companion having to jump in and rescue me. However, her surprised glance, which had immediately turned into a strange look of amusement, caused me to pause momentarily mid-sentence and pass a frantic review over the last few words that had escaped my tongue.

"Chevet," I corrected myself, upon having figured out my own mistake. "Moroni appeared to Joseph at his 'chevet,'" I repeated, intentionally emphasizing the word "chevet" in hopes of replacing the erroneous image that my choice of the word "cheval" must have conjured up in the minds of the young couple we were teaching. It was just a small mix up of sounds—a mix

up which, nevertheless, had the unintended effect of teaching that the angel Moroni had appeared to Joseph "on his horse" instead of at his "bedside."

I made it through the rest of the discussion without earning another look of concern, or amusement, from my companion. Unfortunately, we didn't make it much past the point of asking this young couple if they would like to receive a copy of the Book of Mormon before they emphatically informed us—in a manner that left no room for misinterpretation—that they were not interested.

"Vous américains!" they mockingly brushed us off, mumbling something to the effect that "of course this had to take place in New York. Everything that happens in America takes place in New York!" Immediately I could see the image of tall skyscrapers and busy city streets bursting with taxis and tourists that I was sure had come to their minds. It was the image that most French people had whenever one mentioned New York, or the United States, for that matter. To them, the United States basically consisted of a vast continent with the never-go-to-sleep city of New York on one end and a few sunny California beaches and a big amusement park on the other—with a handful of inconsequential cities and casino-stuffed deserts filling the empty spaces in-between.

After a brief closure to our conversation with the young couple, we found our way to the door and left their tiny, upper-level apartment, and started our descent down the five flights of stairs that separated us from our bikes below. Keenly feeling the sting of the rejection we had just endured, we descended the long, winding stairwell in silence—a silence that was only broken by the reverberating echo of our boots as they clicked against the hard wooden steps. It wasn't until we had finally reached the "rez-de-chaussée" and heard the heavy wooden entrée door snap firmly shut behind us, that my companion broke our reflective silence in an attempt to lighten our discouraged spirits. Rolling her eyes in mock exasperation, she teasingly chided me for my language gaff, causing us both to break into a soul-reviving giggle at the thought of Moroni appearing on a horse. In my defense I quickly countered that in light of the fact that we had been telling this young, disbelieving couple that an "angel" had appeared to a young boy in "New York," the brief moment they were led to believe that the angel was on a horse was probably—in all reality—inconsequential to them.

Even as the words left my mouth and we chuckled once again, the absolute wonder of the message that we were bearing struck me, as if I were hearing it for the first time: an angel had appeared, in our days, to someone just like me. I had grown up hearing the story of Joseph Smith's first vision, as well as the account of the visit of the angel Moroni and had always just believed that it was true. Seeing it from the perspective of this young couple that day, however, caused me to stop and consider just how inconceivable it might sound to someone who had never heard it before.

Propelled into our own thoughts, my companion and I settled back into a silent side-by-side walk as we made our way back to our bikes, passing on the way the solid wall of connected apartment entries—just like the one we had so discouragingly exited—which were occasionally broken up by the door of a tiny specialty boutique or an inviting pastry shop window.

Once we reached the light post where we had secured our bikes, my companion turned to me and broke our long silence with a question that confirmed our matching paths of meditation. "I wonder what our investigators think when they hear the story of the First Vision for the first time?" she queried, reaching mechanically down to unlock her bike as she spoke.

I nodded my head in agreement, sharing with her that I had been thinking about the same thing.

She paused for a moment while I unlocked my bike, then quietly turned to me and asked in all sincerity, "Have you ever specifically prayed to know that the Joseph Smith story is true?"

Her question caught me a little off guard. I stopped a long moment and reflected before I answered. "I can't say that I have," I truthfully admitted, but then added with matching sincerity of my own, "I have just always felt that it was true."

Nodding her head, she acknowledged that it had been the same for her, then added, "I wish that I could know what it feels like when our investigators pray and then learn for the first time that it is true."

My companion's words left me intrigued as I hopped on my bike and pedaled down the street after her. Her question turned itself over and over in my mind. I thought about how, on a daily basis, we taught people how to pray in order to find answers to their questions, and how to know if what we were teaching was true. Diligently we would share with them the promise found in Moroni 10:4 and then invite them to put this promise to the test so that they could know for themselves, through the witness of the Holy Ghost, the truth of all things.

As I pondered on the power of this promise and on the revelatory process, I was cognizant of the fact that my own testimony hadn't come as just

The Answer

one intense answer to prayers, but had come quietly over the course of my life as I had tried to learn and live the gospel of Jesus Christ. I was aware that though I had always had a firm testimony of the gospel, I couldn't ever recall having specifically prayed to have a witness of a particular aspect of the gospel; rather, my testimony had always just been there—an important part of my life—for as long as I could remember, as had been my personal testimony of the power of prayer.

Praying had always been a regular part of my daily life. My dad had always been vigilant in making sure that each morning before he left for work and before we got dressed and scooted off to catch the school bus, we would kneel in family prayer. Throughout my life I had prayed individually for help and strength to make it through personal challenges as well as for special blessings for both myself and others. I had often felt those answers and blessings come. The very fact that I was serving a mission had itself come about as a powerful response to prayer. Yet, I had never specifically prayed to know if the Joseph Smith story was true.

Pedaling along those tree-lined city streets that afternoon, while apartment buildings and local corner cafés blurred past me, I felt a growing desire to be able to experience and to know, in the same manner we promised our investigators would know, that the marvelous account of the First Vision was true. I made up my mind that I was going to ask for that witness in my prayers before retiring to bed that evening.

After what turned out to be a full day of teaching and finding people to teach—and of thinking deeply—I approached my Heavenly Father "à mon chevet" in pajamas that were starting to look a little threadbare at the knees from all the time l had spent kneeling in them since I had begun my mission. I began my prayer almost apologetically, hoping not to offend God by asking for a confirmation of something I felt I already knew the answer to. Carefully, I searched for just the right words to convey the desire that I was feeling in my heart.

At the conclusion of my prayer, I waited expectantly on my knees for some kind of special feeling. Patiently I remained in that uncomfortable position as the long minutes ticked by, shifting my weight occasionally from knee to knee in an attempt to relieve the pressure of the cold, hard floor against them; but nothing came. Finally, tired and dejected, I crawled into bed, slowly pulling the covers up over the head of one very disappointed missionary; I hadn't expected to feel nothing at all.

The busy schedule and appointments during the next few days pushed the thought of my unsuccessful attempt at receiving a personal witness to the back of my mind. As it was, it would be several weeks before my companion and I would have the opportunity to teach the Joseph Smith story, known as the "C" discussion, to another family. When that opportunity came, apparently convinced that I needed a chance to redeem myself, my companion assigned me to teach exactly the same part of the discussion again, only this time admonishing me to "please leave out the part about the horse."

The "C" discussion had been one of the first discussions I had learned as a missionary. It had been spoon fed to me and the other members of my district word for word by our teachers only weeks after we had arrived at the MTC and started our intensive learn-the-French-language-in-two-months experience. During the class (before we began the mind-fatiguing process of memorizing an entire discussion) our teachers went through the discussion line by line, having us mark every liaison, every lift of the voice, every pesky silent letter so that we would be able to recite it correctly and be understood.

Because I was so very new at the language—due to my uninspired decision to drop out of eighth grade French—at first I was stuck memorizing pages and pages of senseless sounds and intonations. Day after day we repeated word after word and line after line of this marvelous account as we sought to commit it to memory—the achievement of which was, for me, another witness that God truly lives and that miracles still exist.

When I had finally finished pasting into my mind every last word of the "C" discussion, the sense of accomplishment was beyond exhilarating. The thought of passing it off to my teacher was not. I was scared spitless. The never-ending night before I was to officially present the "C" discussion to my teacher, I was so nervous that I tossed and turned all night long while visions of botched-up discussions danced mercilessly through my head.

As I met with my teacher the next morning and nervously took my place across from her at a desk in the small classroom where we normally met for class, I was sure she could feel the vibration of my knees as they banged themselves uncontrollably together beneath the desk. Gently she persuaded me to begin, and then—competing with the patience of Job—she picked up her pen and proceeded to listen to me as I butchered the beautiful French

language. Painfully I stumbled over the endless strings of sounds and syllables as I stuttered my way through every word, every line, every paragraph of the discussion until, at last, I arrived at the end.

In the brief pause that ensued, while my teacher attempted to diplomatically touch up the notes she had taken through the course of the discussion, I carefully worked to bring my heart and oxygen intake rates back down to normal levels. After receiving a generous congratulatory "bien fait" and a few kind suggestions, I was then sent off to summon my companion, who I found waiting in the hall— trembling like a leaf—for her turn to present the discussion.

"Piece o' cake," I encouraged her, flashing her a "thumbs up" that I had somehow managed to steady before I floated down the hall on cloud nine and collapsed into a heap of relief.

If I thought it had been a scary ordeal to present the "C" discussion for the first time to my teacher at the MTC, it really had been a "piece of cake" when compared to presenting it for the first time in a small, crowded living room of a real live investigator family. I was certain that the family we were teaching thought they had just experienced some kind of 4.0 magnitude earthquake or something when, upon having finished my part of the discussion, I sank back into the couch and attempted to inconspicuously gain control of my out-of-control knees. However, unlike the congratulatory remarks that I had received from my MTC teacher, I watched—deflated—as the entire family we had been teaching whipped their heads in unison—like a high school pep squad performing at half-time—to find my companion who was seated comfortably on the other side of the couch from me. Making absolutely no attempt to disguise the befuddled expressions that were scrawled across their faces, they begged her to translate for them, explaining that "they didn't understand English."

Needless to say, I spent many hours after that during my individual study time giving the discussions to the expressionless walls of our apartment and to unsuspecting birds and trees from the seat of my bike as I wheeled past them through the streets. Little by little, I was entrusted with the responsibility of presenting more and more concepts to a real live audience, until I was eventually able to make it all the way through a discussion—and be more or less understood—something I managed just fine up until the horse experience.

It had been a few weeks since we had presented that memorable C discussion which, though poorly received by the young couple we had taught it to, had served to send me to my knees at my own "bedside." Although I hadn't received the answer to my prayers in the manner I had sought, I had reflected continually on the wonder of the sacred event of the First Vision since that night.

Such were my thoughts as my companion and I entered the living room of another young family and prepared to teach the "C" discussion—our very first since my uninspired "horse" version of the discussion. Listening to my companion as she gave a brief introduction to the discussion, I felt a deepened appreciation as to how truly remarkable the story we were about to share really was. At the conclusion of her remarks, my companion turned to me and flashed me an "I know you can do this" smile of support. I then began with my part of the discussion. Not more than a few words into my memorized-by-heart account of the Joseph Smith story, I felt a warmth enter into my heart and begin to envelop me. As I progressed through the story, letting those beautiful words spill from my mouth, the presence of the Spirit was so strong. It felt as though my chest were on fire and ready to burst as the Spirit witnessed to me the truthfulness of what was being said. That feeling remained with me throughout the entire presentation of the discussion.

My missionary prayer to know as Moroni had promised was forcefully answered that day, and would be answered, I would find out, by that same unmistakable witness of the Spirit each and every time I would have the occasion to speak or hear the words of that blessed account for the entire rest of my mission.

Post Script

I could feel the wobbly knees of the sister missionary across the desk from me vibrate the floor in the small MTC room where we were seated. She was so visibly nervous I could see her shaking like a leaf from head to toe as she prepared to pass off the "C" discussion to me. It didn't seem that long ago that I had been in that very seat sitting across from my own MTC

The Answer

teacher trying to pass off a discussion in a language that I had been learning for less than eight weeks. It was hard to believe that I was now a teacher there in a dream job—one that I felt so fortunate to have been blessed with upon returning home from my mission.

Trying my best to calm my trembling missionary down with words of encouragement so that we could get started, I poised myself with pen and paper in hand, ready to listen. Shakily she began and I tried inconspicuously to jot down notes that could help with pronunciation and grammar. Her words came out haltingly at best. I found myself silently praying that she would not pass out or shake herself to death before she finished. At times I strained to make out exactly just what it was that she was saying, often only recognizing words and phrases because I knew the discussion so well myself.

I set my pen to the paper in order to make a few notes, and then I felt it—the same warm and powerful feeling I had experienced every time I had given the Joseph Smith discussion on my mission after I had prayed to know if it was true. Reverently, I set my pen down as my heart welled up inside of me, and just quietly listened, bathing in the spirit that had entered the room until this dear terrified sister missionary stumbled through every word and every line. By the end of the discussion, we were both in tears. Once again, I knew my mission prayer had been poignantly answered, and would be, I would come to find out, each and every time I listened to that sacred account for the rest of my life.

"I have . . . prayed many days that I might know these things of myself. And now I do know of myself that they are true; for the Lord God hath made them manifest unto me by his Holy Spirit" Alma 5:46.

CHAPTER SIX

Le Compagnon
The Companion

> "We were not placed on this earth to walk alone. What an amazing source of power, of strength, and of comfort is available to each of us. He who knows us better than we know ourselves, He who sees the larger picture and who knows the end from the beginning, has assured us that He will be there for us to provide help if we but ask. We have the promise: "Pray always, and be believing, and all things shall work together for your good. As we seek our Heavenly Father through fervent, sincere prayer and earnest, dedicated scripture study, our testimonies will become strong and deeply rooted. We will know of God's love for us. We will understand that we do not ever walk alone"(President Thomas S. Monson, "We Never Walk Alone," Ensign, Oct. 2013).

My gratitude ran deep and my satisfaction complete as I stood quietly at the back of a small exposition tent, out of the line of traffic, watching as curious observers slowly circled around our display and stopped every now and then to read the scriptures or look at the pictures we had hung on the walls of the tent. The three questions, "Why am I here?" "Where did I come from?" and "Where am I going?" that had been prominently painted on a three-sided "kiosque" that stood just outside the entrance of the tent, were serving their intended purpose well. Curious fair patrons, lured by the universal desire to know the answers to those soul-searching questions, were

approaching the entrance to the tent that held our missionary display. Then, taking small steps through its flaps, they were quickly glancing around—as if making certain that they weren't going to be trapped inside of some kind of revival meeting from which they wouldn't be able to escape—before they finally committed themselves by coming the rest of the way inside.

I followed each visitor's eyes as they looked around at the exhibit, noticing with satisfaction that they were immediately drawn to the two paper mâché mannequin-like representations of two prophets situated in opposite corners of the far end of the two-roomed tent. There, in one corner of the tent, a life-sized representation of the prophet Isaiah was seated at a small table, holding a writing tool in his hand which rested on rolled-up scrolls of paper spread across the table's surface. In the other corner behind another small table was a representation of the prophet Mormon writing on "Les Plaques d'Or," which had been carefully constructed out of gold-painted cardboard held together with large rings. On the wall between the two "prophets" were scriptural accounts and pictures depicting the coming forth of the Book of Mormon as prophesied in both the Old Testament and the Book of Mormon.

From where I was standing, I could observe the natural flow of the curious

Life-sized representation of the prophet Isaiah created for missionary exhibit.

visitors as their glances left the prophets and then followed the display of Books of Mormon that had been arranged along the wall that led back to the door of the tent. The books had been gathered in as many languages as could be rounded up—with copies in French, German and Spanish being the most prominent as they were the ones most accessible in that particular region. Brochures about the church were stacked neatly at the end of the display, where a few missionaries stood poised, ready to answer questions. Just behind the spot where I stood, in a second part of the tent, a projector had been set up to show a filmstrip about the church for those who "wanted to know more."

The visitors to the fair, once having ascertained that they could freely look at the display—and exit whenever they wanted to—would then follow the display around its three walls, looking at the pictures and reading the scriptures posted there. It was just the effect I had wanted to create when I had come up with the design for this exhibit a few months back. Even though it had been a long, hard, and sometimes lonely road bringing it to fruition, it was well worth the satisfaction I now felt in watching the small crowd of visitors. Perhaps even more significant than that, though, were the invaluable lessons that I had learned in preparing for this fair.

The prophet Mormon is seated left of a picture display depicting the coming forth of the Book of Mormon.

49

Just how my companion and I had ended up with the main responsibility of coming up with the idea for our display remains a mystery to me. All I can remember was that somehow by the end of the initial meeting to discuss a possible entry in the fair, my companion and I had walked away with the charge of doing exactly that. It might have had something to do with the fact that we had been the only ones paying attention and at least offering some ideas as, for some reason, it had taken an inordinate amount of time for the other dozen missionaries—all Elders—to settle down and focus on the matter at hand. Whatever the case, the responsibility—as daunting as it appeared to be—was ours.

The bike ride home from the meeting that night, as well as our next few nightly chats before evening prayer, were replete with the discussion of how we were going to accomplish the pressing task before us. Having been informed that the regional fair was a very popular one—much like our own state and county fairs back home—we were fully aware that having an exhibit in the fair offered the unusual possibility of providing exposure for the church that our city so desperately needed.

As I had dabbled in art and design during my preliminary college experience, the major responsibility for coming up with the design literally fell into my hands. My companion, on the other hand, played an active supporting role in the whole process. Little by little as I sketched, pondered and prayed, an exhibit centered around two "mannequin" prophets started to formulate in my mind. As the ideas started to gel, I began to feel a certain creative excitement at the possibility of carrying out such a project. Still somewhat the "new" kid on the block, I discovered that having something I could do to really contribute to the work energized me. Besides that, "Major Project" had practically been my middle name growing up, as it seemed that I was always happiest when I was right smack in the middle of one.

To be perfectly honest, the idea for the design was in part inspired by an impressive project my kid brother and his buddy had completed a few months before I had left on my mission. One afternoon, bored with whatever it is teenage boys typically find to do with their time, my brother and his friend had decided to use a technique they had learned in their high school art class to produce a papier-mâché mask. By carefully placing layers of tiny paste-soaked paper over the Vaseline-smothered face of a reluctantly reclining "volunteer"—apparently someone who had lost a round of "rock paper scissors"—they had been able to produce a remarkably life-like replica of a human face. A face which, being the teenage boys that they were, they immediately transformed into a very authentic gorilla head. It was a "chef d'oeuvre" which, when combined with the gorilla suit they'd impressively whipped together out of fabric remnants they had found in my mom's sewing drawers, provided them hours of amusement as they chased the neighborhood kids who came to see it—and my mom—around the house. In my mind, it was just a simple process of evolution—in reverse—to turn my brother's idea for a gorilla head into the head, arms and legs of an ancient prophet.

By the next week, having worked every spare minute we could possibly sacrifice from our other missionary responsibilities to work on our project, my companion and I felt very well prepared to present our plans to our district at our next meeting. Eager and excited to get to work immediately on the display, we presented our ideas and then began to hand out assignments to the Elders for projects they could work on. We weren't sure if the low grumbling that resulted was just coming from perpetually empty stomachs, or if it came from a skepticism for our ideas coupled with the fact that it was the sisters who were giving out the orders. All we knew was that our well-intentioned and carefully-thought-out tasks were received about as enthusiastically as chores being handed out by wicked step-mothers to little school boys on a lazy summer day. That initial meeting—which my companion and I were happy to leave early due to a scheduled appointment—didn't go well, to say the very least.

We barely made it out the building and to the safety of our bikes before the tears of frustration we had been fighting began to freely flow. Pedaling a little more slowly than usual, we attempted to buy a little time in order to pull ourselves together and let the breeze of the passing city dry our tears before arriving at the doorstep of our next appointment. After we rang the bell and entered the apartment of the family we were scheduled to teach, we gratefully closed the door—at least temporarily—on what had been a brutally disappointing experience.

The next day, back at the drawing board, I struggled to refine, and to change—if needed—the concept for the display. Anxious that the fair was quickly approaching and understanding the need to get started immediately, I pled for direction as to what to do. I still felt confident that the initial plan involving mannequins would not only work, but at the same time provide a unique point of interest that could draw attention to our exhibit. After I convinced my companion to proceed, we both pressed forward in our preparations so that we could confidently face the Elders in our next meeting.

51

The Companion

At the next meeting, though still met with a bit of resistance from a few pessimistic Elders in the group, my companion and I somehow managed to convince the more willing participants to get started constructing the smaller props for the display. Getting a group of Elders to do arts and crafts, whose hands, for the most part, were much better at pushing balls through hoops on P-day than cutting gold plates out of cardboard boxes, was more challenging than I had at first anticipated. As frantically as a juggler trying to keep twenty balls up in the air, I found myself running from one struggling Elder to another, trying to transmit the vision that I had in my head to his fumbling hands. Try as I might to keep everyone on track, it seemed that as soon as I turned

"Soeur, are you sure this is going to work?"

Always ready to serve in any capacity, Elder Chidester volunteered to be the model for the face, legs and hands. He was stretched out for nearly an hour on a table while we put paper mâché on his face, legs and arms. To make it less painful for when we took the paper mâché molds off of his legs, he had voluntarily shaved his legs and put on a pair of panty hose he bought from the store next to the church. After the session of painting the arms, legs and heads, my companion and I loaded the boxes containing these body parts on to the back of our bikes to transport them home. We got some very strange stares.

The Companion

my back on one group to help another, the effectiveness of the group I had just left would dissolve into a cacophony of distracted conversations about everything and anything except the project we were working on. Added to my already frazzled state of mind was the voice of one persistent dissenter who, seated close enough to me so that I could hear his disparaging comments above the din in the room, seemed to be making a point of repeating over and over again, "This isn't going to work. This isn't going to work."

As a result, by the end of our "work" meeting that day, I was utterly exhausted as well as beyond discouraged, feeling as though I had just spent the past few hours trying to pull a loaded and groaning freight train up the French Alps all by myself.

"Soeur, are you sure this is going to work?" My companion questioned me as we exited the meeting and headed for our bikes. I detected a noticeable trace of doubt in her voice that had been absent throughout the entire process up to that point. Suddenly, it felt as though my last ally had just jumped ship. I didn't have a ready answer for her as I realized in that brief moment that I was no longer sure.

The bike ride home seemed particularly long that night. As I turned onto

Setting up the exhibit.

the street that marked the halfway point to our apartment, the tiny street lamps cast long yellowish shadows on the uneven cobblestones that bumped beneath the wheels of my bike. By then my companion was her usual block or two ahead of me and I was feeling very much alone. Voices of self-doubt and confusion that were already swirling around in my head seemed to grow louder and more convincing with each turn of the pedals. I was discouraged and disheartened, wondering if I had been wasting the valuable time of the missionaries in our district. I felt heavily the responsibility I had been given but didn't know what to do or where to turn.

In desperation I found myself praying aloud from the seat of my bike as I pedaled along. "Help me know what to do," I pled. "Help me so that I won't waste the precious time of all the missionaries in this district—so that I won't waste Thy time—if what I have come up with won't work."

The prayer had barely left my lips and I had only pedaled a few blocks further when a quiet, but sure, impression filled my pleading heart.

"Keep going. You are not alone. I am with you." The soft, reassuring voice filled my mind as if it had come from deep inside of me. "You can trust what you feel," it whispered to my doubting spirit.

Almost instantly, a humbling peace distilled upon me. With unmistakable clarity, I was made to know in that very moment that as long as God was with me, it didn't matter who else was—or in this case, was not. Filled with the peaceful assurance that He would guide and strengthen me in carrying out this heavy responsibility, I pedaled the rest of the way home renewed in the confidence that with Him, I was never truly alone, and that through Him I could do absolutely anything. Even make papier-mâché prophets.

The voice of a woman who approached me where I was standing in the tent brought me suddenly back to my senses. Apparently having finished her self-guided tour of the display tent, and catching sight of my missionary name tag, she curiously questioned me, "Could you tell me what your church believes about God?"

"I would love to," I answered, moved by the deep sense of gratitude I felt welling up in my heart for a loving Father I had recently come to know even better.

55

Post Script

A few months after my decision to make the big move from a singles' ward into a family ward, I was called to be the Young Women's President. Having decided to basically leave the other YW leaders in their current callings until I could get better established, I was the newest kid on the block in every sense.

Not too far into my calling, I perceived a very real need for improved spirituality in our little group of girls. Having grown up in an incredibly active young women's program–which had not only been instrumental in strengthening my testimony, but had also been the means for reaching out and bringing other young women living on the fringes into full activity—I felt that some things could be done a little differently in an effort to try and improve the overall spiritual quality of our meetings and activities.

Night after night, I prayed fervently for direction as to what could be done, and as a result, I felt prompted to implement a few changes in the focus of our weekly activities to better reflect the intended purpose of those activities. It was a change, however, that was met with a bit of undisguised resistance. As I proceeded to make some of the changes I felt were necessary, I felt like a one-woman band trying to rally the grumbling troops. Little by little I began to feel myself noticeably on the outside of the very group I was supposed to be leading as I tried to set things on the path I felt we needed to be taking. Discouraged, I found hope in the fact that I was going to be able to spend a few days at Girls' Camp that summer, thinking that this experience might help to change things for the better.

I had always had a special love for Girls' Camp, having spent a week of practically every summer of my post-Beehive life immersed in that potentially life-changing environment.

Year after year I had witnessed the power of that grimy, smoke-filled week in the mountains which somehow had the magical ability to transform spiritually reluctant souls into weeping, testimony-filled circles of hugs and tissues. Now as a YW leader, I looked forward to a similar few days in the mountains, praying that it would bring us all together and light a spiritual fire in the hearts of my little group.

However, from my observations of the first few days of camp, it wasn't happening. The spiritually renewing firesides around the flames of a glowing campfire that I had hoped for just weren't taking place. Instead, the circles that did form were often spent exchanging complaints and stories that bordered on being inappropriate—in any circle. It seemed that any effort I made to change the direction of things, including pulling out my guitar and strumming primary songs—which had always instantaneously seemed to work in the past—was met with general disinterest or in some cases, distinguishable resistance.

I started to doubt my ability to lead this group, as it seemed everything I tried only widened the gap I was starting to feel. I wondered if my years in a singles' ward had somehow warped my perspective on what I should expect in "a grown-up world" and if the rules of interacting with the youth had somehow changed in my absence. Feeling so very alone, I began to doubt myself, and in particular to doubt the voice of the Spirit inside of me. I felt so utterly lost in this "new" world, not knowing what I would do if I could no longer depend on that guiding voice that I had come to rely on so heavily for guidance. Needing some time to sort it all out, I headed for my own little grove of trees so that I could pray.

The Companion

I retreated to a quiet, secluded area far enough away from the clatter of voices that filled the smoke-filled campground, in order to find a spot where I could kneel down and pray. I felt confused and very much alone, doubting both myself and the voice I had been trying to listen to inside of me.

Tearfully offering up the concerns of my heart, I asked to know what I should do. As the tender reassurance filled my heart that my prayers were indeed being heard, and that a loving Heavenly Father was guiding me—and that I was not alone—I remembered a lonely bike ride through the dimly lit streets of France and paper mâché prophets. I headed back to camp sometime later, renewed and confident that with God as my companion, not only could I help Elders produce prophets out of paper and paste, but that I could do this as well. I felt assured that with His divine help—and through the words of living prophets—He would guide me in what I needed to do in order to help to bring about a spiritual evolution in the hearts of these young girls.

"Be strong and of good courage; be not afraid, neither be thou dismayed: for the Lord thy God is with thee whithersoever thou goest" Joshua 1:9

CHAPTER SEVEN

Mes Anges
My Angels

> *"We never need to feel that we are alone or unloved in the Lord's service because we never are. We can feel the love of God. The Savior has promised angels on our left and our right to bear us up. And He always keeps His word"* (President Henry B. Eyring, *"Mountains to Climb,"* Ensign, *May 2012).*

hadn't meant to be reckless. Generally, I was pretty good at navigating my bike through the narrow space that separated the idling cars waiting impatiently at the "feu rouge" from those parked bumper to bumper—in true French fashion—along the side of the road. I had also invented a kind of a game—a sort of personal challenge—to see just how long I could go at each red light without having to put my feet down in order to catch my balance before the light turned green. In all modesty, I was actually getting quite good at maneuvering tight squeezes and then waiting—perfectly balanced, with my feet still on the pedals—until the light changed. Except for this time. As it was, I probably could have picked my way through this particular challenge as well, had I happened to notice the large mirror protruding from the side of the parked truck on my right before I did—which happened to be about two seconds too late.

The jolt of my handlebar crashing into the long arm of the truck's mirror quickly sent my bike catapulting towards the car in the lane on my left, causing me in turn to catch the mirror on the side of that car with the other handlebar. Only this time, instead of just bouncing off as I had done with the truck, to my horror, the impact of my handlebar somehow managed to dislodge the entire

mirror mechanism from the car, sending it crashing down to the asphalt below where it landed with a sickening thud. Stunned, I cast a furtive glance at the window on the passenger side of the car only to catch the glaring disbelief on the face of the occupant seated there. It was quite obvious that she was not the least bit amused. Timidly, I bent down to pick up the damaged mirror from off the road, hoping above all hopes that my long, straight hair would somehow hang in such a way as to temporarily obscure my mission badge from view; after all, perhaps this was not the best moment to remember my missionary duty and ask this disgruntled passenger and the driver in the seat next to her if they would "like to know more about the plan of happiness."

Before I could even straighten all the way up and choke out some sort of apology and offer to somehow pay for the damages, an angry arm shot out of the window—which had been hastily lowered. Its grip snatched the mirror right out of my unsuspecting hands. The hand-cranked window was then furiously raised. In a gesture of disgust, the car and its occupants sped off, huffing through a light that my guardian angels had mercifully turned a bright green for me—just in the nick of time.

I wondered when they would give up on me, those guardian angels I was sure had been assigned to take care of me on my mission. Admittedly, I had kept them plenty busy dashing here and there as I blissfully pedaled my bike through the streets of France, dodging speeding cars and trying to avoid flying over the handlebars when the tires of my bike hit railroad tracks at just the wrong angle.

Before I was a missionary, I hadn't thought much about how Heavenly Father answered everyone's prayers and took care of all of us there were to take care of; I just knew that somehow He did.

Now, after several months of being out in the field, in a strange new land far away from the protective care of a father and mother who had watched over and protected me all my life, I had perceived, from time to time, the subtle presence of a protective heavenly force around me. It was a sort of quiet recognition that came to me, like a gentle breeze fluttering across my spirit that let me know when I had just received some kind of extra help and when somebody or something was helping to keep me safe; it wasn't really anything I could see or touch—it was just something I could sense.

On one of my long bike treks across town, as I passed groups of rushing people on the sidewalks, and carfuls more weaving around me on the cobblestone streets, my mind started to wander as I began to contemplate how it was possible that God could know all these individual people, and more importantly, answer all of our prayers. As I mulled the question over in my mind for a few miles, I was struck with the thought that the work of heaven must be accomplished, much like it is here on earth, with organizations of people assigned to look out for the welfare of each other; only in heaven, it involved organizations of God's angels assigned to help Him look after the affairs of those of us still passing through our mortal probation. The idea made perfect sense to me, resonating quietly with my spirit. As I pondered the possibility further, my mind was enlarged with the understanding that those "personal angels" assigned to look after, to help, and sometimes to even save us mortals are most likely our very own ancestors—our grands and greats who know us, and who love us.

That marvelous insight rested so sweetly on my soul as I contemplated this wondrous possibility. At that moment, although I knew that I was very far away from my physical home and the family who had watched over me, nurtured me and loved me, I could rest assured that I would be safe, warm and protected in the loving care of my angels—departed family members that I would one day meet again.

Post Script

Some years after my mission, I found myself accompanying my mother and father on a trip back to Philadelphia, the city of their birth. As new converts to the church, my parents had moved their young family west in order to raise their children closer to the center of the church. As a result, I had spent most of my life separated–by what amounted to an entire continent–from my grandparents and anyone else to whom I was directly related.

The day I visited, for the first time, the grave site of my grandmother in a church cemetery located not far from the center of Philadelphia, I took a single rose that I had purchased from a nearby florist to place on her grave. My parents and I entered

My Angels

the small fenced cemetery through a creaky iron gate located at the side of the church and started the daunting task of systematically going row by row through the graveyard, searching for the tombstone carved with my grandmother's name. It was apparent that many of the tombstones had been in that little cemetery for years, as some were leaning and worn with age, making it hard at times to read the names they bore.

As we moved from grave to grave, to my surprise, it occurred to me that the cemetery was filled with row upon row of family names I had grown up hearing about: Simon, Hoffner, Singley, Shisler. Every now and then, I would hear my mom exclaim, "Oh, that's uncle so and so," or point in another direction and announce, "That is a distant cousin," or "I think this is a family name." Somehow, standing in that small cemetery with my parents on that bright summer day, I felt strangely at home in a place I had never been before.

It was such a new experience for me to be surrounded by people to whom I was related in some way, never mind the fact that none of these people were alive. At that moment, my heart was turned, as is stated in Malachi 4:6, to "the hearts of [my] fathers" and I felt the overwhelming desire to learn about and to write the story of my family.

Upon returning home, I began the lengthy task of gathering together everything I could get my hands on that would help me learn about my ancestors and attempt to tell the stories of their lives. Staring at the boxes of old faded pictures, and pouring through all the obscure dates and facts I had accumulated, I felt my heart fill with a spirit of recognition as though I was meeting and getting to know, again, beings that I had already known and loved. As their names and lives became familiar to me, I found myself often wondering, "Which ones of you have been assigned to be my personal angels? Which ones of you did I feel there with me as I performed my labors as a missionary in far-off France? Which ones of you have been with me, throughout my life, guiding me, guarding me and sometimes even saving me?"

Sometime later, I had the precious experience of going to the temple with my family members to perform the temple ordinances for some of our kindred dead. As I entered those holy temple doors, tenderly carrying in my hands the cards that bore the family names I had been assigned to take through the temple, my heart was filled with a deep sense of reverence. I couldn't help but think that very possibly among those names of departed family members were the very names of some of those who so lovingly had watched over me and had kept me safe throughout the years; with a heart full of love and gratitude, I knew it was now my turn to watch over them, and to do the work that would eventually save them.

"For he shall give his angels charge over thee, to keep thee in all thy ways" Psalms 91:11.

Sister Jackson South Carolina Columbia Mission, 2014

My Angels

Sister Jackson and missionaries from the Thailand Bangkok Mission tour an ancient city, 2014

CHAPTER EIGHT

La Promesse

The Promise

{
"When you were set apart by priesthood authority, you received the right and privilege to represent the Lord... Do not be afraid or shy about fulfilling this commission. Just as the sons of Mosiah, you are to teach with the power and authority of God ("What Is My Purpose as a Missionary?" Preach My Gospel: A Guide to Missionary Service, *2004. 1–16).*
}

My companion was, might I say, not amused as we lay in a tangled heap on the tiny landing at the bottom of a staircase. The long, slippery wooden banisters that wound themselves up and around the stacked flights of stairs that led from apartment to apartment had long been a temptation for me—a temptation I had dutifully resisted, until then. But that day had seemed like such a perfect day for a celebratory ride down one of them. I must admit that when I'd daintily hopped up onto my awaiting mount—in proper English sidesaddle fashion, of course—and before I had bravely let go of my grip on the round wooden knob at the top of the banister, I hadn't given much thought as to how I might stop once I arrived at the bottom.

My descent down the slippery slope was quicker and wobblier than expected. Only seconds after my joy ride had begun, it came to a screeching halt as I crashed headlong into my companion on the bottom step. The collision sent both of us both sprawling to the floor. It was immediately obvious upon impact that the whole experience had been much more of an adventure for me than it had been for my companion.

As I carefully picked myself up to a sitting position, apologizing profusely to my companion, who was still lying on her back, I struggled unsuccessfully to stifle the rising giggles that were escaping somewhat uncontrollably from my throat, threatening to severely undermine the sincerity of my apology. Nervously, I glanced back at the door at the top of the stairs—a door that only seconds before had gently closed, ending the spiritually rich discussion that we had just enjoyed with the young couple who lived behind it. I hoped above all hopes that the commotion I had caused wouldn't result in the door swinging back open to expose our less-than-dignified position at the bottom of the stairs. It was a day for much rejoicing—perhaps to be celebrated in a different manner than I had chosen—but a day for rejoicing nonetheless.

My heart was full to bursting with the manifestation of the Lord's hand in His work that my companion and I had witnessed that day in the home we had just left—a manifestation of promises made and of promises kept. Over the weeks of meeting and sharing the truths of the gospel with this young family, we had been able to see the precepts of the gospel slowly begin to settle themselves into their hearts and to miraculously change their lives. We had witnessed one of those miracles today.

It had been readily apparent since the beginning days of my mission that the commandment to live the Word of Wisdom could pose a bit of a problem for those I might teach in France—a country filled with people whose very heritage is so closely linked to their love for, and almost worship of, the fruit of the vine. Evidence of this proud French product and tradition is visibly manifest throughout the charming French countryside as row after neat little row of beautiful, meticulously manicured vineyards stretch across kilometer after kilometer of rolling hills.

Even if you were a teetotaler, or missionaries like we were, some kind of a drink was always poured for you—or at the very least offered—each and every time you sat down in someone's home, even if it was just for a few minutes. Our hosts would often become perplexed after trying to offer their entire list of preferred liquid refreshment such as "le café, le thé ou les boissons alcoolisées." They would finally set before us—almost apologetically—a lightly flavored glass of syrup water, which always came minus any trace of ice.

At first it took some time to learn to appreciate and then to actually like this barely cold, barely flavored water as it strangely resembled a weak drink in which the ice had melted and diluted the flavor. There was, however, plenty of opportunity to acquire such a taste, as any "petite boisson" once placed before you would quickly become a bottomless drink that would be dutifully refilled each and every time it reached half empty—a tiny matter which could pose a teeny bit of a problem for a missionary who was out on a bike all day long. After all, free French restrooms were even more scarce than French ice cubes.

As a result, it was part of the missionary "savoir faire"—as well as a necessary part of daily survival—to figure out just how to make the first drink you were poured last precisely until the discussion you were presenting was done—save a few last swallows you could reserve until just before bidding a final "au revoir." It was a strategy that generally worked, unless of course the conversation took on a whole new direction, and all empty glasses would be generously filled once again.

Sitting in the living room of this young couple that particular day, having finished our syrup-flavored water—except for the last few sips—we essentially challenged them to renounce their naturally inherited French traditions and abstain from partaking of any of the harmful substances mentioned in the 89th section of the Doctrine and Covenants for what amounted to the rest of their lives. In doing so, I sensed heavily the weightiness of our request. I understood clearly the awkwardness such a change could pose for them both in their own families and in their social circles. I also understood the difficulty it often is to change well-established routines and habits. Though not heavy drinkers themselves, the couple acknowledged that wine and alcoholic beverages played a part in many of their family and social gatherings as well as in their holiday celebrations—which, it turned out, were just around the corner. In addition to that, the husband was and had been a smoker for most of his life—an addiction he freely admitted that he had tried to rid himself of, but had never been successful in doing. The Word of Wisdom was a challenge not to be taken lightly, and one that would require a lot of determination and commitment.

A long moment of silence followed our challenge as the couple first looked at us and then at each other. Then, with great hesitancy in their voices, they apologetically informed us that they might consider the challenge sometime in the future, but thought that it would be better to wait until after the holidays. They explained that if they decided to make such a commitment before the holidays, that it would be hard—if not impossible—to keep it, considering all the social activities and parties that generally took place during that time of year.

For a long moment we paused, taking in what they had shared with us while at the same time understanding the enormity of what we were asking them to do. It would have been an easy task at that point to agree with them, except for the fact that the Spirit was so powerfully and undeniably dictating otherwise.

Gently, but with a resolution prompted by the heavens, we proceeded to challenge this young couple to begin immediately to live the Word of Wisdom. The effect of this boldly delivered challenge registered itself instantly on both of their faces and in our senses. Nevertheless, prodded on by an undeniable impression, and with a boldness of speech that was not our own, we issued with the challenge a promise, and did so as representatives of the Lord Jesus Christ. We promised them that if they committed to live the Word of Wisdom and were able to be completely obedient to it throughout the upcoming holidays, then the Lord would bless them in such a manner that it would never again be an issue or a struggle for them.

Silence hung in the air for quite some time, but finally when they did speak, they agreed—though somewhat apprehensively—that they would exercise their faith and accept the challenge we had given them to start living the Word of Wisdom that day.

It had been a bold promise, one that had taken a lot of faith and trust to make. However, both my companion and I reverently concurred, as we pedaled our bikes side by side and discussed the whole experience on our way home, that the Spirit had placed that promise in our mouths that day. As daunting as it may have seemed in the moment to declare such a bold and binding promise—a promise whose fulfillment, or lack of, would be so unmistakably evident—the fact remained that we had both felt the undeniable prompting to make it. And so we had.

The rest of the journey home was one of quiet introspection for me as I fell back into my usual position behind my companion, overcome with a sense of the sacred trust and responsibility the Lord had given to us as His missionaries to represent His mind and will. I felt humbled at the sacred trust and responsibility He had given to me—a young girl just barely into my twenties who only months previously had been just another college student struggling to work my way through school. As I reflected upon what I had been called and entrusted to do as a missionary for the Lord Jesus Christ, I experienced a humbling sense of wonder at the responsibility I had and of the commission I had been given.

The holiday break seemed endlessly long as my companion and I waited for our next appointment with this couple. Each morning and evening as we waited to meet with them again, we would ask in our companion prayers that they would be able to be strong in keeping the promise and commitment they had made to live the Word of Wisdom. On the day of our long-awaited appointment, we anxiously climbed the winding stairs up to their small apartment, all the while trying diligently to fan the flame of our faith and believe—as we had promised—that they had been able to keep the Word of Wisdom despite their many holiday celebrations.

They greeted us warmly and invited us to sit with them in their small living room as they generously poured for us two tall glasses of syrup-enhanced water. After a few exchanges of some "comment-allez-vous" followed by a few minutes of small talk, we got right to the point.
"How did you do with your commitment to live the Word of Wisdom?" we asked expectantly.

Without a moment's hesitation, but with some wonder in their voices, they both readily admitted that they had been able to do it, adding that it had been much easier than they had anticipated. In humble gratitude, we acknowledged that they had just witnessed the loving hand of the Lord in their lives—as had we.

Post Script

It was in a different house, and on a different sofa that I sat some fifteen years later as I joyously reunited with this couple on a return visit to France. I had looked forward to this visit with great anticipation. Having kept in touch over the years, I had learned that though the husband had not been baptized at the same time as his wife—she had been baptized only a few months after my companion and I had challenged them to live the Word of Wisdom—he had finally joined the rest of his family by entering into the waters of baptism.

As we caught up on each other's lives and talked about our experiences since the last time we had seen each other, the subject of the husband's original problem of smoking somehow came up. Casually he mentioned how some years ago

The Promise

one of his colleagues, who had observed how he had managed to completely quit smoking, had asked him for some advice as to what he could do to also rid himself of this habit.

"I didn't know what to advise him," he candidly admitted. "All I could tell him was that after many years of trying to quit, one day I just quit and never again had the least desire to pick up another cigarette."

I could tell by his recounting of his ability to completely walk away from a nagging habit that had plagued him for so many years that the genesis of that victory had somehow managed to fade from his memory. But it hadn't from mine.

"I think I just might be able to help you remember how you were able to do that," I reflectively contributed, thinking back on a very slippery banister on a special day of celebration—a celebration of kept promises.

"For the Holy Ghost shall teach you in the same hour what ye ought to say" Luke 12:12.

My companion, Sister Popham, the eternal prankster. She left love notes on the bikes of the Elders in my name and short-sheeted my bed the last night of her mission.

CHAPTER NINE
La Guerre
The War

> *"No pain that we suffer, no trial that we experience is wasted. It ministers to our education, to the development of such qualities as patience, faith, fortitude and humility. All that we suffer and all that we endure, especially when we endure it patiently, builds up our characters, purifies our hearts, expands our souls, and makes us more tender and charitable, more worthy to be called the children of God. . . . And it is through sorrow and suffering, toil and tribulation, that we gain the education that we came here to acquire and which will make us more like our Father and Mother in heaven"* (Spencer W. Kimball, "Tragedy or Destiny," Brigham Young University Speeches of the Year. 6 Dec. 1955).

"It was that apartment building right over there that the Germans overtook and made into their headquarters," the gentle Madame Reeb explained as she pointed her wrinkled, time-worn finger towards the window of her third-story apartment and directed our attention to another apartment building situated right across the courtyard from hers. She was a kindly lady who never spoke a word unless it was coated in a genuine layer of love and kindness—a kindliness that was keenly felt each time my companion and I were invited to sit down and share the truths of the gospel with her in her tiny front room. But there was a certain unfamiliar edge to her voice that day as she began to recount to us some of her less-than-kindly memories of "la guerre."

71

"It was just over there by the park that I saw the ragged and hungry French soldiers being held prisoner by a German guard," she continued, moving her hand ever so slightly to the left until she was pointing at a popular public park located just across the street. My companion and I knew the park well. It was a beautiful park, filled with flower-lined walks and meandering creeks. Tall lean posts topped off by large nests of native storks peeked above the trees that dotted the well-manicured gardens of the park. On several beautiful spring days my companion and I had strolled along its endless walks, meeting and greeting the people who were relaxing there.

As the memories came flooding back, Madame Reeb's eyes took on a distant stare as if envisioning painful scenes from another lifetime. "I was just returning from the 'boulangerie' that day when I saw the soldiers sitting there lined up against the fence, so hungry and cold. The German guards had their guns pointed at them and were yelling for them to be quiet."

It was hard to imagine this beautiful city held captive by the heavily armed German soldiers who had marched their thundering boots through these tranquil cobblestone streets and brandished their death machines at the slightest provocation during those long months of their occupation. Yet the residue of such nightmarish days was still very present even decades after the un-welcome strangers had retreated back to their side of the Rhine. Aging veterans—living souvenirs of the war's human devastation—walked and often limped through the streets, many still displaying their dangling war medals proudly pinned to their chests. Shining testaments of heroic deeds, these medals told the stories of otherwise common folk who, turning hero, had risked life and limb for their fellow countrymen and for freedom. Throughout the city, unrepaired bullet holes and scarred sections of crumbling walls still remained in some of the older churches and buildings, standing boldly as an ever-present reminder of exactly what the people of this town, and this country, had suffered at the expense of their neighbors.

I'd been stunned when I had first learned just how incredibly close in proximity these once-battling neighbors really lived to each other. On one of my first P-days as a missionary in the city of Strasbourg, my companion and I had ridden our bikes to the banks of the Rhine river and, with the other missionaries in our district, had enjoyed a peaceful picnic in a small war memorial park located there. Following our picnic, we had examined the concrete and steel remains of a bunker that had defended the city during the war. Then my companion had directed my attention to the opposite shore of the river and indicated "That's Germany." She then had added, "If you walk to the middle of the bridge, you are in Germany."

Gazing across the modest width of the river, I had been able to plainly see the homes of the people who lived there and had thought that if I but strained my eyes a little more, it would be possible to see the face and perhaps even the eyes of someone standing on the other side. It seemed incomprehensible that these two great enemies in such a destructive and deadly war could live so close to each other as to practically be able to look each other in the eye. I couldn't imagine what it had felt like during the war, or what it felt like now, to know that your former enemy, who at one time had taken away your freedom, ravaged your home and country and snuffed out the lives of people you knew and loved, was only separated from you by an insignificant ribbon of water.

"I had only been able to buy one baguette of bread at the 'boulangerie,'" Madame Reeb continued on with her story, "and that was supposed to last my family for a week." She described how food had become so scarce during the German occupation that it had had to be rationed. When she described the pitiful condition of the disheveled French soldiers being held prisoner by the German guards and how one of them had cried out like a hungry child for "un petit morceau de pain," I could sense in her a renewed indignation at seeing fellow countrymen being treated in such an inhumane manner.

"I couldn't just walk by a hungry French soldier without giving him some of my bread," she declared, "so I broke off a piece of bread and offered it to him." The same kindness and compassion that defined her very character had returned to her voice.

Yet her eyes darkened as she began to explain what had happened next.

"One of the German guards screamed something at me in German," she recalled, trembling as if the experience had just happened the other day instead of decades previously.

Then with horror rising in her voice, she described how the guard had immediately swung the gun he was holding around until it had pointed directly at her. Other German guards surrounded her, forcing her to a sitting position beside the soldier she had just fed. Terrified and panic-stricken, she waited, not knowing what would befall her.

My companion and I sat riveted in our chairs as fragile, kind Madame Reeb reflectively recounted the unbelievable details of what had happened after that. We learned that eventually she was transported to a work camp where she would remain imprisoned until the end of the war. Through the many

The War

months she was a prisoner in the camp, she was nearly starved and forced to endure many other inhumane treatments along with the other helpless women in the camp.

"But all that is done now and France is free, and so am I," she concluded as she picked up a delicate handkerchief that had temporarily rested in her lap and continued to carefully crochet its lace-like edges.

It was hard to believe that gentle, compassionate, faith-filled Madame Reeb had lived through all of that horror and had survived to tell about it. It was poignantly powerful to observe how, after having suffered so much, she could come back to her peaceful home and once again cheerfully sit by the window overlooking the park below and talk about the goodness of God. Unlike so many others, she did not blame God for the atrocities that had been forced upon her or upon her world, but rather she thanked Him daily for having helped her to endure through the hard times.

Watching how Madame Reeb had faithfully put into living practice the lessons she had learned about God and life during those difficult times, I learned volumes about the human spirit as well as its ability to gracefully survive and conquer even the most difficult circumstances and hardships. And, too, her courageous example taught me volumes about facing one's enemies.

Sister Ashcroft, Salt Lake City West Mission, 2013, struggles to free her entangled skirt. She was only able to free herself when the bottom of her skirt ripped off.

Post Script

"Look at those tall nests!" an excited student exclaimed, pointing out the window of the tour bus as the bus slowed down to pass by the beautiful sprawling city park. We were on the tail end of a marvelous tour of northern France that had taken us, among other places, from the beaches of Normandy to the battlefields of Verdun. Whenever I could, I had tried to make sure that a visit to Europe would include a close up and personal reminder to my students of just what so many had paid for the price of freedom.

"Those are storks' nests," the tour guide on the bus explained amid "ooohs" and "ahhs" that issued forth from the other students once they too caught sight of the nests. "Storks are considered to be the symbol of the town and live protected in this park," the guide continued, pointing out the right side of the bus at the park that I knew so well.

My attention, however, was drawn to the other side of the bus where I gazed reflectively upon a tall apartment building. In my mind I could still see Madame Reeb, who by then had long since passed on, still sitting by her window. I have never forgotten the history lessons I learned at her feet, nor the lessons I learned about making it through the hard times that would eventually come into my own life.

"Isn't life good?" I could hear her say, as she smiled and her eyes twinkled with loving kindness and forgiveness.

"Yes it is," I found myself quietly agreeing, "Isn't life good."

"But the fruit of the Spirit is love, joy, peace, gentleness, goodness, faith" Galatians 5:22.

The War

Sister Greenwood, Sister Mullen,
and Sister Peterson
Thailand Bangkok Mission
2014

CHAPTER TEN
Le Cantique
The Hymnal

{ *"Few joys in life are sweeter and longer lasting than knowing that you have helped others take the restored gospel of Jesus Christ into their hearts"* (Henry B. Eyring, *"How Great Shall Be Your Joy,"* Liahona, *Feb. 2011*). }

The day almost started out as a disaster. For some reason my companion and I just couldn't get out of the apartment without forgetting something else we had to go back for. When we finally got on our way, the baptism was to start in just thirty-five minutes—which posed a bit of a problem as it generally took us at least that much time to bike the distance to the church house where the baptism was to be held. We prayed for green lights and a clear route and I'm sure we came close to breaking the land speed record for bicycles as we pedaled as fast as our little missionary legs could take us.

As soon as we arrived at the church house, disheveled and out of breath, we hastily threw our bikes down, fastened them to the first thing we could find that wasn't moving, and sprinted into the small church building. To our dismay we discovered that the baptismal font had not yet been completely filled; it had only just barely been uncovered, having been concealed under the floor of the small general purpose room of the church house. Feigning a calm that neither of us were feeling, my companion and I greeted the clearly nervous young mother who was to be baptized that morning and assured her that everything would be taken care of. Then desperately, we both offered silent prayers that it would be. Needless to say, this was not the way I had imagined my very first baptism in the mission field would be like months before, when I had first stepped off the plane ready to convert the entire "francophone" world.

Frantically working the small crowd of members who had gathered to attend the baptism, my companion and I first tried to find out which priesthood brother was in charge of the baptism and then tried to find the man himself. We found out that he was not even there yet but was speedily "en route" as he had somehow forgotten that there was to be a baptism that day. I felt sick and worried about how this day, which was to be so monumental in the life of this dear sister, had begun.

Within minutes of the arrival of the person in charge, the waiting members were quickly set in motion to make the necessary preparations for the baptism. Unfortunately, in the interim, the tiny gang of young children who had accompanied their parents to see the baptism, had gotten restless. Noisily they chased each other around the room. I wondered if things could get much worse as I looked desperately around the room for anything I could do to remedy the situation.

Out of the corner of my eye, I spied a branch member holding the guitar she had brought for me so I could play a musical number with her later in the program. Silently I thanked the heavens that I had learned to play the guitar at a young age and had spent many starlit nights around countless Girls' Camp fires trying to calm excited Beehives by strumming and singing every possible Primary song that existed until the girls could be tucked safely into bed. Knowing that if I had to, I could play for hours, and aware that we needed to do something fast, I gathered the children together and we started to sing. We continued to sing every song I could think of until the Spirit began to fill the room.

When the baptismal program finally began, and the newest convert of the branch was led down the steps into the font, I marveled at how remarkably simple the baptismal ordinance was. No clanging of bells or tooting of horns. Just a simple prayer and then a symbolic ordinance of death and rebirth. I reflected upon the countless hours of teaching and testifying that had preceded this act, the lifelong habits and hearts that had been changed, the prayers that had been offered, the faith that had been exercised—all leading up to this one uncomplicated, yet eternally significant event. It was simple, yet beautiful. It was simply beautiful.

While I knew that this was only the beginning of this sister's journey back to the Father's Kingdom, and that what happened in her life from this point on was what would matter in the end, I felt an assurance in my heart that the angels of heaven had witnessed her act of obedience and rejoiced that another daughter of God had chosen to set her feet on the straight and narrow path and begin her journey home.

Post Script

It felt like a dream to be sitting in the home of this sweet sister some twenty years later. She stood leaning against the doorway listening as I strummed the guitar in an attempt to teach one of her teenaged daughters some Primary songs in English. Without a word, she slipped out of the room and returned with a somewhat tattered hymn book that she quietly placed in my hands. It took me a few seconds to fully understand what I was holding, but when I did, tears came readily to my eyes. Although worn and dog-eared from years and years of devoted use, I recognized the hymnal as the gift my companion and I had given to her following her baptism on that almost disastrous day. It seemed strange to know that the last time I had held that book in my hands I had been a missionary.

Slowly I turned the first page and caught sight of my own handwriting declaring my testimony next to that of my companion's. I couldn't say a word for a moment while my heart took it all in. The well-worn book seemed to be a symbolic testament that this sister's life had been fully devoted and dedicated to the service of the Lord. It was evident that the book had accompanied this good sister to church for many years as she had righteously raised her family of three children with a husband who had eventually joined his baptismal covenant with hers. It had been with her through all those years that she had selflessly served the members of her branch and eventual ward as a president or counselor of one organization

or another, calling after calling. It now stood as a witness that her feet had not wandered, but were moving ever forward along the path she had chosen to follow so many years ago by that one simple yet beautiful act of baptism.

As I reverently handed the book back to this sweet sister—and eternal friend—I couldn't help but notice the light of a beautiful soul shining brightly through her smiling eyes. The words came haltingly at best as I attempted to place meaning on all that I was feeling. My heart, full to bursting, overflowed with gratitude at having been able to share in such a sacredly memorable moment. The unspeakable joy I felt in knowing that I had been able to play even the tiniest part in introducing God's plan of happiness to this dear sister and her family was truly great—greater than I had ever known.

"And if it so be that you should labor all your days in crying repentance unto this people, and bring, save it be one soul unto me, how great shall be your joy with him in the kingdom of my Father" Doctrine and Covenants 18:15.

Sister Pope, England Birmingham Mission, 2010

CHAPTER ELEVEN

Les Soldats

The Soldiers

{ *"The secret to enjoying true freedom in life is learning how to truly desire to do the things you are called on to do in life" (Sister Jacquelyn Parker, 1976, Brussels Belgium Mission Conference).* }

"Bonjour mes chers frères et soeurs" the sometimes gravelly, and always southern-Utah-farm-girl-flavored voice of our mission mom rang out from over the pulpit. Sister Parker's presence always inspired our attention, just as it did then as she prepared to address the missionaries during our six-zone Mission Conference. It had been an exciting few days of inspirational and motivational meetings as the northern part of our mission had met in Brussels for the conference. A bit like General Conference, Girls' Night Out and Christmas all rolled up into one, a mission conference was not only a chance to receive the gift of a much needed spiritual re-charge, it also provided a joyful, missionary-appropriate back-slapping and hand-shaking reunion with the other missionaries you had served with throughout your mission experience.

As an additional bonus, it was also an opportunity to spend some time with other sister missionaries. As it was, "Les Soeurs" were generally assigned only one team to a city, which meant that there were times sister missionaries could go for months on end without ever even seeing another missionary who didn't have the first name of "Elder" and who wasn't wearing a suit and tie—and who wasn't always hungry.

Even though it was a wonderful experience working side by side, and occasionally feeding, all those valiant, spiritually maturing young men—future fathers, bishops, stake presidents "en herbe" whom were loved like brothers (most of the time)—it was exceptionally gratifying and rejuvenating to just be with other sisters. There was something incredibly comforting about being with missionaries who, along with performing all their other missionary duties, knew what it was like to have to sometimes stifle a giggling attack from erupting or to hold back a threatening tear—or a few—and do it all in addition to laboring diligently to keep a skirt safely tucked in while buzzing around town on a bike.

All eyes and ears became riveted on Sister Parker as she prefaced her remarks in the same reflective manner with which she had begun so many of her talks. "I've been thinking about..." —an introduction which always caused you to feel as though you had just received a warm and personal invitation into her deeply profound and meditative thought process. Her reflective insights on life had always lifted and inspired me throughout my mission whenever I had had the opportunity to hear her speak. As I prepared to receive her message that day, I was keenly aware that I was in dire need of some of that lifting inspiration at that particular point in my mission.

It had been a difficult past few months for me. Leaving my greenie city of Strasbourg where I had spent the first six months of my mission—the city where I had fallen in love with my mission and with the people of my mission—had been harder than I had expected. Considered to be the "apple of the mission's eye" with its beautiful cathedral and quaint Alsatian architecture, my first assignment had been without a doubt "la destination populaire" for all of the missionaries.

As I had departed that beautiful city "en train," I had waved a tearful "au revoir" to the small group of missionaries and members who had come to see me off. Somewhat naively and in an attempt to console myself, I'd simply told myself that the next phase of my mission would bring more of the same. A six hour train ride later, I discovered how very different the same mission experience could be. I didn't know it then, but the next few months of my mission would make up some of the most demanding and "mettle-testing" weeks and months I would experience as a missionary.

I perceived an immediate scenery change the moment I gathered my belongings together and stepped off the train into the dense, heavy, gray ocean air of my new city to greet my new companion, who inauspiciously was not there. After a few moments of anxious waiting and looking around for any-one who might in the least bit resemble a sister missionary, I set out to find her. Clumsily I made my way through the crowded train station, juggling my bike and the large suitcases that I had stuffed to the brim with all my earthly missionary possessions. I hadn't advanced too far before I gratefully caught sight of two Elders who were quickly approaching me. They greeted me, then mumbled some sort of explanation under their breath as to why my compan-ion wasn't there before they gathered up my belongings and led me towards the exit.

I hadn't gotten more than a few steps past the large exit doors before I was greeted by a mysterious person who jumped out at me from behind a large col-umn. "Boo!" the jumping figure cried out with all ten fingers raised in the air to complete the effect. Confused, I quickly caught sight of the familiar missionary badge and realized I was meeting my next companion who, I would find out—true to my very first impression—was an eternal prankster.

It was evident, however, that she was not joking the next day as we pre-pared for companion study and I casually asked her about the people we were teaching.

"We aren't teaching anyone," she flatly informed me.

I'm sure my face registered my immediate bewilderment as I blankly stared back at her, too surprised by her unexpected answer to make any at-tempt in hiding my astonishment.

"No one, as in "personne?" I clarified, wanting to make sure I hadn't mis-understood what she had said.

"Yep," she responded, "No one."

Even though in my previous city, my companion and I had had nowhere near the weekly teaching opportunities that my friends who were serving in South American missions were having (who sometimes sounded as if they were having a hard time keeping track of all the people they were leading to the waters of baptism) we at least had had some regular investigators that we met with and taught either on a weekly or bi-weekly basis. Just having one spiritually charged meeting with someone who was the least bit receptive to the message of the gospel had the effect of erasing the discouragement of a multitude of closed doors, as well as hours and hours of unsuccessful contact-ing one might face in a day, or in a week. I couldn't imagine what it would feel like to go days on end with no one to teach. I soon found out, however, just what that was like.

83

After an unsuccessful week full of long hours of going "porte à porte" and of attempting to contact people in the street, I felt exhausted yet still managed to remain optimistically hopeful that eventually we would find somebody to teach. Nevertheless, I could readily sense how this steady diet of less-than-successful people contacting must have worn on my companion, who had just six months left in her mission and was keeping a not-too-subtle day by day countdown of just how much time remained. Already having served in the same city for four months and two companion changes before me, it was no secret that she was more than a little anxious and expectant of seeing that special little letter arrive from the Mission Home on transfer day with her name on it. At times, I wondered if the poor "facteur" —who month after month on that particular red-letter day continued to leave my companion standing empty-handed in the foyer by the mailboxes—knew just how close he had come to receiving bodily harm each month.

I really couldn't blame my companion for wanting a little scenery change as I was quickly learning that the progress of the church in that particular industrial port city seemed as bleak and gray as its weather and as the history many of its inhabitants had endured. Critically situated along the French coast, this little town had been a target of German fury during World War II, a fact that remained evident from the bullet-ridden buildings and endless war memorials that greeted us around every corner. Many of the buildings leveled during the war had been hastily replaced with cheap concrete structures that essentially contributed to the bleakness of the town and had the effect of completely effacing just about any trace of the quaint older-than-history ambiance that generally characterized the center of French towns and cities. The older inhabitants of this town had suffered a lot at the hands of foreigners, which led to their hesitancy to open their doors and their hearts to strangers—and to us.

A bright spot of the transfer occurred on the first Sunday when I was finally able to meet the members and the other four missionaries we would be working with that made up the sum total of our branch and missionary district. Seeing the "salle" that served as the branch's meeting house, however, was not one of the more bright spots. The members, though few in number—thirteen regular attendees to be exact, with most of them coming from one family—were humbly devoted saints, nourishing their faith on what was essentially the bare bones organization and offerings of the church. The missionaries that formed our district were all hard-working and devoted as well. The "salle," on the other hand, needed a lot of work.

I got my first look at the apartment building, whose second story floor served as the meeting place for the city's small branch of saints, when my companion and I pulled our bikes to a stop and dismounted them in front of the well-time-worn building. Noticing the black plaque mounted to the side of a green weather-blistered entry door indicating that this was the meeting place for "L'église de Jésus-Christ des Saints des Derniers Jours," I couldn't help but notice as well that this converted apartment building had seen better days.

A musty smell tickled my nose as we pushed open the heavy door and wheeled our bikes into the small stair well where we locked them up before mounting the worn and creaky stairs leading up to the second floor. Passing through the door on the second floor, we entered the "grande salle" which, when set up with several rows of hard fold-up chairs, served as the chapel. Upon inquiring, I soon learned that the building had originally started out as a private school for girls, but then had been used as a prison for soldiers during the war. Though members of the small struggling branch had done the best they could with their meager resources to make this a suitable house of worship, I was not entirely convinced that much had changed in the general condition of the building since the time it had served as a prison.

In the weeks to come I would sometimes find myself more than a little distracted during our sacrament meeting as I subconsciously washed, scraped and painted—in my mind—all the peeling walls and time-worn floors over and over again. In doing so, I couldn't help but think of the beautiful buildings back home that I had so often taken for granted in my home state of Utah: nice, clean chapels dotting the horizon every few blocks as far as the eye could see. I sometimes wondered how much of an obstacle this humble meeting place might pose for an investigator—once we had one—upon attending church here for the first time.

I found I wouldn't have to worry about that for quite some time, however, as the next sometimes painfully long days stretched themselves into long weeks that were filled with a steady diet of endless hours of tracting down countless streets in fatiguing humid heat without a trace of success. Very quickly I discovered that my companion and I, while overly wealthy in time, were poverty-stricken in finding anything to do in all that time, except tract. Increasingly, as the days dragged on, it became more and more difficult to keep myself enthused and motivated when so many hours of thrusting in the sickle only left us empty-handed and didn't produce so much as a single, tiny fledgling seedling to nurture and to watch over.

The Soldiers

Somewhat guiltily, I soon found myself resisting less and less the long and sometimes mindless bike rides that were spent chasing down "call backs" or people who had expressed a remote interest, but who could never be found home after that. It seemed that the route to check on these call backs —which was charted out in our planning meetings each morning—was often planned to crisscross back and forth across town in such a way as to use up as much of our overabundant time as possible. Facing day after day, and week after week of hastily closed doors and sometimes hostile or belittling residents who showed little or no interest in talking to us, I was led to weakly wonder after one particularly discouraging day how many more months I could really do this.

Disheartened and spiritually exhausted, I felt heavily the bonds of my missionary duty. It didn't help that my very healthy and persistent conscience had also jumped on the bandwagon of discontentment by constantly reminding me of what I could be doing in order to be a better missionary. As I felt my personal commitment and enthusiasm start to wane, I prayed daily for the strength and the discipline I needed to just keep doing what I knew I needed to do. Pleadingly, I prayed for the motivation to put my sometimes faltering heart back into the work. Sister Parker's talk in our mission conference meeting was, in part, a blessed answer to that prayer.

The theme of her talk was based on the scriptures found in the Doctrine and Covenants in chapter 58 verses 26, 27 which speak about being an unprofitable servant. Immediately I related to that scripture in a way that I never had before —knowing only too well what it felt like to be unprofitable. Our mission mom spoke straight from her heart as she addressed us, which was always exactly what we had come to expect from her. What you saw with her was always just what you got: no pretenses, no putting on airs, just pure, straight-forward, 100% sincere, and personal.

Asking if she might be able to share with us some of the insights that had come to her as she had been pondering the meaning of these scriptures, she told us about her eldest son who at that time was attending an American high school in Brussels. Explaining that her son had decided that he wanted to play on the high school football team, she added that this wasn't just a casual decision, but something he wanted to do with all of his heart. She commented on the fact that she had never seen him so excited about anything.

Day after day she observed how her son, who was motivated by his intense desire to make the team, fully engaged himself in not only doing what the coach required of him in his daily workouts, but in doing everything in his power to ensure that his name would be on that final roster when the time came to announce the team. As a consequence, in addition to those mettle-testing practices his coach put him through, he followed a very demanding personal two-hour conditioning program every day just to make sure he would be good enough for the team. Making the observation that one would think her son would quite naturally have reason to complain about how tired and overworked he felt, Sister Parker noted instead that he never did. Not even for one tiny second. Instead, he absolutely loved and reveled in every minute of his difficult workout and couldn't seem to do enough. In her words she insightfully suggested that "He was free, free, free—free as a bird." And eventually profitable, she also noted.

The analogy was clear and sank deep into my heart as Sister Parker contrasted how different things might have been had his heart not been fully set on making the team, or if he had joined the team simply because she and her husband wanted him to play football. She admitted that while he would have probably still done it and gone through the workouts—just because he was an obedient son and would want to please his parents—it would have nevertheless been a completely different experience for him. Had that been the case, those very same grueling workouts—which he would then dutifully endure and perform day after day—would become hard and burdensome maybe even to the point of being insufferable for him. She was certain that even though he would still dutifully accomplish what was required, he would probably do just what was expected and no more, all the while anxiously counting down every tick of the clock until his required workout was finally over.

"The secret to being truly free, and to finding true joy in your service, and in your life," Sister Parker concluded at the end of her carefully thought out analogy, "is in learning how to put your whole heart into what you are doing. True freedom is found in learning how to find the desire to be doing the things that you must do in life."

Her powerfully personal message penetrated my weary missionary heart. I left that conference feeling renewed and ready to thrust back in the sickle with all of my might. I returned to my little port city ready to give my heart back to the Savior—only this time, all of it.

Over the next few weeks after the conference, I sensed a marked difference in the manner in which I approached the work. Once again, I felt the energy seeping back into my work as I dug in, totally engaged and fully committed to do my best. I could tell my companion was feeling the same as

the quality in how we used our time slowly began to improve along with the effectiveness of our contacts.

On one bright summer afternoon, instead of facing a hastily closing door, we stared at one that warmly opened up even wider, followed by an invitation to come in and share our message; I knew that the long drought was finally over and that the promised harvest had begun. The long hard battle had been won. My grateful heart was full and I felt free, truly free at last.

Post Script

" God be with you till we meet again," our small gathering of former Brussels Belgium missionaries sang out in French with weepy, tear-filled eyes as we stood in a tight semi-circle at the rear of the chapel. It was the conclusion of a beautifully tender funeral service for our beloved mission mom, Sister Jacquelyn Parker. The service had been a moving tribute to the life of a grand lady who had been the source of inspiration for so many of us in attendance that day, and especially for the group of her former, noticeably aging missionaries who now stood to honor her. We had changed so much over the decades since we had last stood together as missionaries that we hardly recognized each other without the aid of the missionary name badges we had so long ago retired.

But for that one brief moment as we stood united together once again in final tribute to a dear life that had touched us all, and one that had motivated and mothered us through some of our most difficult challenges, we knew forever and always that we were Brussels Belgium missionaries, and that we were hers.

"Dieu soit avec toi," the final notes of the song rang out as the added voices of the rest of the congregation, singing in English, joined in on the last two verses. In my heart, I added a most personal and heartfelt "Merci" to one who had lifted me in my hour of need by helping me find the path to true freedom.

"For behold, it is not meet that I should command in all things; for he that is compelled in all things, the same is a slothful and not a wise servant; wherefore he receiveth no reward. Verily, I say that men should be anxiously engaged in a good cause, and do many things of their own free will, and bring to pass much righteousness" Doctrine and Covenants 58:26-27.

Sister Jackson and Sister Powell
Texas San Antonio Mission
2014

Sister Larrabee
Texas McAllen Mission
(Spanish Speaking)
2014

CHAPTER TWELVE
L'invitation
The Invitation

{ *"When I . . . realize that the Father promises to all his sons and daughters who are willing to pay the price of keeping all his commandments that he will give unto them all he has, I feel that it is indeed worth the price" (Elder M. Russell Ballard, "Is it Worth it?" Brigham Young University Fireside, 2 Sept. 1979).* }

It had been a long, hard day of going "porte à porte." Strangely, it always seemed that once we started knocking on doors at the top of a street, suddenly no one was home on the entire rest of the block. The current street we had just finished tracting was no exception. How all those people, who we had just seen scurrying to and fro from their apartment buildings, had so quickly disappeared is most certainly one of the great mysteries of the kingdom. Even those perpetually present white-haired ladies, who spent their days lazily leaning out their shuttered, geranium-lined windows and curiously watching those passing by below, were gone.

Somewhat discouraged, my companion and I returned to the corner where we had locked our bikes and started wheeling them out to where the small neighborhood joined the main street. Just before reaching the corner, we passed by a tiny, meticulous yard bordered by a low white wooden fence. No one had answered the door the first time we had tried this house, but this time we noticed an elderly lady who seemed to be in her late 70's stooping down to pick something up in the front yard. We called out an amiable "bonjour" as we pushed our bikes past her gate. She straightened up, smiled and then surprised us by walking towards us rather than hurrying off in the other direction to the safety of her home.

"Vous n'êtes pas d'ici," she keenly observed, obviously catching our American accents. Politely she inquired as to what had brought us so far away from home and into her neighborhood. We replied that "we were representatives of Jesus Christ with a special message to share." To our surprise, instead of suddenly throwing up her hands in that typical French gesture that clearly communicates "I don't have the time to be bothered by whatever you want to bother me with," she remained fixed where she was, smiling expectantly, as if encouraging us to continue.

It only took a few minutes with this kindly lady to feel the special spirit she emulated. It was evident that she loved the Lord and welcomed any opportunity to talk about Him. Prompted by the Spirit, which was so abundantly present, we asked if we might be able to share a story about an important book of scripture with her. Warmly, she invited us into her home, which opened up into a miniature kitchen with a table barely large enough for the three of us to crowd around. As we sat huddled around her table and began to share with her the marvelous account of the restoration of the gospel and the coming forth of the Book of Mormon, the Spirit was so tangibly present and powerful I felt as though I could reach out and touch it.

That was the first of many such wonderful visits to come, as it became somewhat of a routine for us to make a weekly visit with "Madame Vanhille," as we had come to know her. At each visit, shortly after our arrival, she would quietly excuse herself and quickly disappear through a small trap door that opened up from the kitchen floor into a small cellar below. A few moments after having descended, she would hurriedly emerge, carefully balancing three small bottles of "Schweppes" soda in her arms, which she would then place on the table next to the tall glasses and straws that she had set out ahead of time. The time would fly by as we sat there sipping and sharing the precious truths of the gospel with this gentle lady, lesson after lesson. Our hearts were always filled to bursting during the bike ride home as we reflected upon those spirit-filled visits with our dearly loved "petite grand-mère" as we had come to call her, to which she would always affectionately respond, "you are my keeds," in her endearing French accent.

Over the next few lessons, it became apparent that things were progressing to the point for us to challenge Madame Vanhille to be baptized. Normally, this should have felt like such a joyous occasion, especially for a missionary who was working in a city where finding somebody to teach—let alone inviting them to be baptized—was about as rare as finding water in the Sahara Desert. Curiously, however, instead of feeling joy at the thought of asking Madame Vanhille to be baptized, I was beginning to feel a tremendous turmoil inside.

The question as to whether or not Madame Vanhille loved and served the Lord was not the source of my turmoil, as her love and devotion to Him was evident in her every word and action. Getting Madame Vanhille to pray was not a problem either, as praying was as important and natural as breathing was to her. Faithfully, she attended her own church, read the scriptures, and even followed her own code of health which resembled very much our own. She was, to use a phrase my dad would often employ, "a dry Mormon." Nevertheless, my turmoil was so very deep and real that it would not leave my heart or my mind.

As I slowly pedaled my bicycle away from another wonderful discussion with Madame Vanhille, I struggled with all my might to discover the source of this unusual disquiet I was experiencing. Deep in my thoughts, I was unaware of the black city that blurred past me on that long ride home that night. I reviewed in my mind how, over the course of meeting with Madame Vanhille, we had come to know and to care a great deal about this gentle little lady.

We had learned that, while she had no living family members, she was nevertheless not alone in this small town; wonderful, caring members of her own church, "angels on earth," would faithfully stop by each and every day to visit with her, making sure that she was surrounded by friends and that she had the things she needed. They would drive her to the grocery store, take her to the doctor and accompany her to church. They would see also to it that she was not lonely, but instead watched over by fellow parishioners who made sure she was encircled by their love and friendship. I realized, as I reflected on the feelings that were consuming me, that my conflict came in considering how Madame Vanhille's baptism and her ensuing membership in the small, struggling branch of only a handful of members could possibly change all of that for her.

As I thought about those humble members of the church, I wondered who among them would be able to look after this gentle, sweet lady in the same manner that the members of her own congregation so faithfully did. As it was, there was not one member of the branch who lived anywhere remotely near to Madame Vanhille, and only one member who even owned a car. The

The Invitation

member who did own a car happened to live miles away on the outskirts of the town in the opposite direction from Madame Vanhille's little "quartier." Try as I might, I couldn't figure out how she would even be able to attend church were she to become a member. She lived too far away from the building where the branch met to walk there. Despite the efficient public transportation systems generally found in most French towns and cities, there was not one single bus that Madame Vanhille could take on Sunday that would drop her off anywhere near the building where church services were held.

The longer I thought about it, the more conflicted my emotions became as I imagined the possibility of Madame Vanhille, "ma petite grand-mère," all alone, with no one to care and look after her—a stranger in a new church in the evening of her life. It felt like a gigantic battle between my heart and my soul as I struggled to come to terms with how I was feeling. On that reflective bike ride home that evening, I prayed so desperately to know what would really be best for dear Madame Vanhille.

It felt so very foreign to even have this conflict going on inside of me. So many questions swirled through my mind as I pedaled silently through those quiet streets that night, that I felt as though I had temporarily become the investigator, instead of the missionary. I found myself pondering in my mind the very same questions my companions and I had answered at least a million times for the people of France—questions for which I felt I already knew the answers. Yet they continued to swirl through my mind as if I were reviewing them for the very first time.

"Why did Madame Vanhille need to change religions when her life already seemed so close to being right before the Lord?"

"Why wasn't her baptism, which had been performed in her own church—by immersion—good enough?"

"What exactly is it that Madame Vanhille would gain by leaving the loving congregation of the church she belonged to, in order to join the struggling branch in the city where I served?" The endless drumming of questions churned over and over in my mind to the repetitive turning of the wheels. Finally, my mind hit upon the question at the base of my conflict. With all the sincerity of my soul I questioned, "Would the blessings Madame Vanhille receive be worth the sacrifices she might be called on to endure in what remained of her earthly life?" I knew I needed to know the answer to that question before I could invite Madame Vanhille to be baptized; I knew I needed to know the answer for her, and for myself.

As I continued pondering, pedaling and praying for peace and for answers, the resonating words "One Lord, one faith, one baptism" kept recycling themselves through my mind to the alternating rhythm of my pumping feet. I meditated as well on the meaning of the verses that proclaim that the path that leads to the Kingdom of the Father and all that He has "is strait and narrow and few there be that find it." As those sacred words circled themselves through my heart and through my head, their meaning finally found place in my conflicted heart. I understood with deeper clarity than I had ever before experienced that the thrice repeated word "one" really didn't leave any wiggle room, not even for a close second. Coupled with that understanding came the forceful conclusion that in order for sweet and faithful Madame Vanhille to inherit not just some, but all of God's blessings, her feet needed to be set upon the strait and narrow path—something that could only be done through baptism into His true church by those to whom He had given proper authority.

As those sacred words filled my mind, I felt the calming presence of the Holy Spirit quietly and gently begin to settle my heart. My mind then turned to a joyful scene. I envisioned a smiling, radiant Madame Vanhille passing through the veil at the end of her mortal existence and being welcomed into the loving embrace of a rejoicing family and a loving Savior—never to be alone again. At last comforted, I finished that ride home with a new-found peace and assurance that the joy that Madame Vanhille would then feel as she knelt before her Savior surrounded by her loved ones in God's presence—the joy that we can all feel one day as we kneel before our Savior having followed the path He trod—would be worth any price we might have to pay in this life. With renewed clarity, I also understood that until that glorious day, God would take care of those who love and obey Him: that He would take care of Madame Vanhille.

I never got the opportunity to extend the blessed invitation of baptism to Madame Vanhille, however, as the news of my unexpected transfer came before my companion and I had the opportunity to teach her again. Devastated at the thought of leaving my job undone, and with only a brief moment to stop by and offer a quick and tearful goodbye to "ma petite grand-mère," I boarded the train with a heavy heart for my next city.

Throughout the next few months of my mission, I tried to make contact with the two new sister missionaries who ultimately replaced both my companion and myself, as my companion had come to the end of her mission not more than a month after my transfer. To my dismay, I found out that by the time

The Invitation

the two new sisters had finally started going back to visit Madame Vanhille, the decision had been made to completely remove sister missionaries from that struggling little city. As a result, there was no one left who was even aware of all those wonderful hours that had been spent sharing the gospel with a lovely little lady in a tiny kitchen over a bottle of Schweppes soda.

Over time, having only received a letter or two in response to the several letters that I had written, I eventually lost touch with Madame Vanhille. Nevertheless, I thought often of my dear little "grand-mère" and the things she had helped me learn about God's plan. I wondered what eventually became of her, and how much longer it had been until she passed to the other side and knelt before her Savior. I could only hope that in the precious time we had sat with her around her tiny kitchen table sharing with her the marvelous truths of the restored gospel, we had prepared her to recognize and to embrace the gospel when she finally got that chance—and that she would remember the truths that her "keeds" with the funny accent had taught her.

One thing I knew for certain was that she had helped prepare me for my life and for the sacrifices I would be called on to endure in the days to come. I knew that I could face them all with the utmost confidence. That any price I would have to pay in this life in order to follow the Savior would ultimately be worth it.

Post Script

One Sunday morning, while reading through my missionary journal, my thoughts were turned once again to my dear Madame Vanhille. Though it had been a long time since I had taught her as a missionary, I had never forgotten her. Later on that morning, during Fast and Testimony meeting, I listened to the sweet testimony of our ward's Family History specialist about doing the work for the dead. Madame Vanhille's name flashed through my mind. Silently calculating in my head the years since my companion and I had taught her, it came to me that unless she had lived an inordinately long life, "ma petite grand-mère" had most assuredly already passed to the other side. I caught my breath as the thought occurred to me that there was some work that I had left undone.

Almost as quickly as the startling prospect of having Madame Vanhille's work done for her entered my mind, the discouraging realization came to me that I didn't even know her first name, as my companion and I had always addressed her by her last name. As I searched my mind for a first name that I had only briefly seen decades ago, suddenly the name of "Georgette" impressed itself upon my mind. "Her name is Georgette," the Spirit whispered to me, and I knew immediately that was it.

Quickly I scrawled a short message on a torn-off piece of paper and passed it to the sister who had just born her testimony, asking if she could find anything on "Georgette Vanille"— I didn't realize at that point that I had been misspelling her name, having forgotten that there was a pesky silent "h" in it. Upon receiving my note, this dear sister looked back at me and nodded a smiling confirmation. Briefly we met after the meeting and I shared with her the story behind the note.

"I'll see what I can do," she assured me.

Not more than a few hours after our initial conversation, I heard my phone ring and recognized the excited voice of the sister with whom I had spoken.

"I found it!" she excitedly exclaimed. "I had to find it through a back door, but I found it!" However, she added, "I need to tell you. I think you left out a silent 'h' in her name." I remembered that "h" the minute I heard about it feeling a sudden rush of joy at the thought that she had indeed found my dear Madame Vanhille.

The Invitation

Tenderly, I took the record in my hand. Quick tears came to my eyes as I realized on reading the date of her death, that she had passed from this existence only five short years after my companion and I had taught her. My heart filled with gratitude as I felt as though I had been given a second chance to try and somehow finally deliver the long delayed invitation to my "petite grand-mère," and thus complete my missionary duty.

"One Lord, one faith, one baptism" Ephesians 4:5.

Sister Plumley and
Sister Schmuhl
Brussels Belgium Mission
1993

CHAPTER THIRTEEN

Le Plan

The Plan

> *"The Spirit of God speaking to the spirit of man has power to impart truth with greater effect and understanding than the truth can be imparted by personal contact even with heavenly beings. Through the Holy Ghost the truth is woven into the very fiber and sinews of the body so that it cannot be forgotten"* (Joseph F. Smith, Doctrines of Salvation, *3 vols. 1954–56. 1:47–48).*

t had been a hard sell even getting through the front door of this elderly couple's home. For what seemed like hours, my companion and I had stood on the front porch trying to convince the wife that we had an important message for her and her ninety-year-old husband to hear. Emphatically, she explained to us that her husband had listened to many teachers of religion, but that they had never convinced him of anything. She was pleasant enough, but assured us that we would just be wasting our time trying to teach him anything new. In a last-ditch effort, we'd asked her if we could just try our luck and see how we did. Smiling, she'd moved aside and showed us in. As she led us into the living room and pulled up some chairs for us, she wished us luck and then disappeared into a side bedroom to summon her husband.

After a few moments she reappeared, followed by a smiling, white-haired, gray-stubbled man who could have been anybody's grandpa. Slowly he limped forward to where we were seated and shook our hands before plopping himself down in a well-worn rocking chair that was obviously his.

"The wife says you think you can convert me to your religion," he said, leaning forward in a challenging sort of manner with an unmistakable mischievous twinkle in his eye. "You know I've had many teachers of religion over the years try and talk to me into believing in their religion, but none of them have convinced me yet. So what makes you think you can?"

With that, my companion and I began offering one approach after another in an effort to find a lead-in so that we could begin to teach a lesson. It felt as though we were playing cat and mouse with the elderly man who seemed to be holding all the cards in the game. Playfully he led us all over the place—up and down one dead-end street after another—obviously enjoying the game he was skillfully playing with us. Amused at a scene she had evidently been witness to more than once, his wife sat quietly by as the match continued.

As my companion took her turn at trying to find an approach that would work, I looked around the room and happened to catch sight of an old, faded photograph of a young girl, perhaps in her twenties, that was propped up on the long mantle-piece before me.

"Is that a picture of your daughter?" I curiously asked the couple, when my companion finally paused to reload.

Suddenly the entire mood of the room changed and went eerily quiet. The looks on the faces of both the man and the wife seemed to transform instantaneously from playful to painful. We sat in momentary silence before the wife answered my question.

"Yes. She was our only daughter. She died when she was twenty-three."

Quickly doing the math in my head, I estimated that it had been at least thirty years that their daughter had been deceased. I was moved that the grief at her early departure was still so very poignant in the faces of this elderly couple as if it had just happened yesterday.

Suddenly, enlightened by the undeniable presence of the Spirit, words began to fill my mind and spill from my mouth that spoke about the Plan of Salvation and how they could one day see and live again with their daughter. When I paused to take a breath, my companion picked up, continuing on in a seamless, yet completely unrehearsed transition. It was nothing like the mostly memorized, but spirit-felt discussion that we generally gave when teaching the Plan of Salvation, but was instead a spontaneous explanation that seemed to be spoon fed to us by the Spirit as it poured forth from our mouths. On and on my companion and I spoke, alternating turns without a detectable pause in-between, one picking up right where the other one had left off in what felt like a finely prepared monologue. Only it wasn't. The French rolled eloquently and effortlessly from our tongues as we shared concept after concept about the eternal nature of families and the Savior's loving plan to allow us to live together forever with our families.

I can't remember all that was said or how long we talked. All I can remember is how I felt—the incredible burning that filled my bosom—and the heaven-inspired look I detected on the faces of this elderly couple. It appeared as if they were having an open vision just above our heads as they sat riveted, taking in every word. I wondered what marvelous things I might have seen had only I turned my head to look.

Finally, with the message delivered, the outpouring ended. While the Spirit still reverently filled that small living room, my companion and I humbly testified as to the truthfulness of what the Spirit had taught us that day—what it had taught all of us.

A hushed moment of silence ensued. Then, quietly, in a voice that was not much above a whisper, the elderly man finally addressed us.

"You have spoken with the tongues of angels, like at Pentecost," he proclaimed in a reverential tone.

Then, mirroring the words pronounced by King Agrippa after having been taught by the apostle Paul, he continued, "Presque vous m'avez convaincu" (Almost thou persuadest me). The words hung in the air like a sacred testament of what we all had just experienced.

We didn't stay much longer after the bearing of our testimonies and the offering of the closing prayer. After having set another appointment to come back, we quietly left, not wanting to dilute in any degree the powerful outpouring of the Spirit that we had just witnessed.

Silently we pushed our bikes along the narrow street, lost in our own quiet reflection for quite some time before either of us spoke a word to each other. Even then, it was difficult to know what to say that could describe what we had both experienced, so we continued on in silence, letting the testimony of the words that had been put into our mouths permanently etch itself into our souls.

The Plan

Post Script

" Families can be together forever through Heavenly Father's plan." The notes of the beloved primary song quietly floated across the stillness of the frosty air as my family huddled around the graveside of our beloved father. Although it had been several years since had we tearfully laid him to rest, his absence in our hearts and in our lives remained tenderly keen.

As a family, we had made it our yearly ritual to meet there on the day that commemorated my dad's birthday, laden with white balloons and messages that we would release into the heavens until they disappeared from view.

As the last notes of the song faded and we said our final farewells to each other, I stayed behind, lingering a moment in reflective silence. My mind went back to a quiet afternoon in a tiny living room of an elderly grieving father and mother, when as a young missionary, I had felt the Spirit bear powerful witness through me and my companion as to the eternal nature of families. As I stood there at my father's grave on that cold winter day, I understood with a comprehension made even more profound by my own life's experiences, the glorious sense of hope and joy that I once saw reflected in the eyes and on the faces of that couple on that memorable day so long ago.

"O death, where is thy sting? O grave, where is thy victory?"
1 Corinthians 15:55

CHAPTER FOURTEEN

La Pluie

The Rain

> *"I like to look for rainbows, whenever there is rain. And ponder on the beauties of an earth made clean again. I want my life to be as clean as earth right after rain. I want to be the best I can, and live with God again"* (Nita Dale Milner, "When I am Baptized," Primary Children's Hymn Book. *1998. 103*).

The rain began to fall and I pulled one of those cheap plastic rain bonnets from out of my pocket and offered it to the stylishly dressed member walking beside my companion and me. It was the kind of bonnet that grandmas and little children sometimes wore back home and which we always kept tucked in our pockets for such an occasion.

"Non merci!" the member refused without reservation. She was about our age, and had readily agreed when we had asked her to accompany us on some of the scheduled visits we had for that day. We were used to being out in the rain sometimes all day long. Apparently she wasn't. The quick and resolute manner in which she refused our efforts to help her keep her head dry—in a storm that was becoming more and more serious by the minute—made it plenty clear that we had insulted her sense of French fashion with the offer.

I was long past the stage of my mission where I had considered fashion over practicality. Admittedly, there had been a brief period near the beginning of my mission when I had watched with interest—and a tiny sense of condescending amusement—as my companion had prepared herself to go out, especially on cold days. Fastidiously, she would rifle through her half of

the corner "armoire" where the sum total of her missionary wardrobe was hanging and carefully pick out whatever articles of clothing looked the warmest—and smelled the most clean. Then she would proceed to pile on an often uncoordinated array of clothing, layer after layer over the double layer of tights and thermal long johns that she wore underneath, until she got to the top layer—which she would make sure matched, most of the time. On especially cold days, her ensemble would be completed with a pair of knee-high leather boots which were insulated by two pairs of socks and empty plastic lunch bags—if we had any—that she would carefully wrap around each foot before she slipped them into the boots. At the end of the day, she would reverse the process, peeling off layers like a human banana, instantaneously losing twenty pounds in the process.

At first, it was also hard not to notice—with my fresh from the college scene eyes—how worn my companion's clothes seemed to be, especially around the backside where they rubbed against the seat of the bike, and how their colors seemed quite faded in comparison to my fresh-out-of-the suitcase missionary outfits. It was a difference that I found quickly disappeared, however, after not too many weeks of wearing the same sets of clothing day after day and exposing them to the weekly torture of public laundry facilities. It also didn't take very many bone-chilling bike rides in the humidity-intensified cold air of France to change my perspective and to help me decide that it didn't matter so much what I looked like, or how many layers of uncoordinated articles of clothing I put on over my double layer of tights and newly acquired long johns—or what I wore under my knee-high leather boots to insulate them—as long as I was warm and relatively dry.

Even more importantly than that, I came to realize over time that the regular soak-to-the-skin spring and summer rain showers along with the chill-to-the-bone humid winters were the price that I would have to pay in exchange for the beautiful, lush green French foliage that I had come to love. It also came to me, after a period of getting to know the elements so close up and personal, that there was a certain freedom that came from occasionally just letting go of the natural reaction to protect oneself from the rain, and just enjoying it—enjoying the sound of it splashing against the cobblestone walks and roads and experiencing what it was like to just walk, or bike, splashing through puddles as carefree as a school-aged child. Then there was also that certain rejuvenating, fresh "je ne sais quoi" earth smell that would tickle my nostrils on its way to filling my lungs each time I took my first breath of newly-baptized "terre." At times it was like receiving a heavenly soul-quenching drink of water.

The coastal city where I served at the time had provided my companion and me with plenty of opportunities to "drink from the well of heavenly refreshment" and to splash through the rain, as a mid-morning deluge was nearly a daily occurrence. The day we were accompanied by our bonnet-resisting accomplice was no exception and soon she became soaking wet, yet consistently "à la mode."

At the conclusion of our appointment, we dropped her off at the safety of her dry house just minutes before the heavens burst open and drenched my companion and me to the core with another celestial bath. As we splashed our bikes through the quickly gathering streams of water that formed along the sides of the roads, we did our best to avoid becoming victims of the spraying jets of water that would shoot out like geysers from beneath the tires of passing motorists.

Once arriving at the street in front of our apartment, soggy and dripping, I remembered a letter I had recently received from one of my friends who was currently serving her stateside mission from the cushy seat of a mission car. After learning that I was riding a bike during my mission, she had innocently inquired in her next letter to me, "But what do you do when it rains?"

Knowing that a picture was worth a thousand words, we talked a passerby into taking one of us before we sloshed in to our apartment in order to dry off. Soaked to the bone and drenched from head to toe—except for where our cheap plastic rain bonnets clung listlessly to our partially protected heads—we stood, side by side, holding onto our bikes with smiles, which spread blissfully across our dripping faces from one soggy ear to the other.

"This is what we do when it rains," I playfully scrawled across the back of the picture before I carefully placed it in an envelope, licked the flap and sent it on its way to my friend in dryer parts of the world. All the while I smiled to myself with the thought that I just might be sharing one of life's greatest secrets.

The Rain

Post Script

There was a lot on my mind as I pulled the door closed to my house and slowly turned the key in the lock. My head was filled with heavy thoughts of the responsibilities that faced me at work that day. As I turned towards my car parked in the driveway, I felt tired and lacking the energy and motivation I felt I needed to get through all I had to do that day.

Before I could even catch sight of the telling evidence of rain still clinging to the leaves of the trees and notice that the sidewalk beneath my feet was damp, my unsuspecting lungs drew in the fresh fragrance of a newly fallen rain. I had been totally unaware of the fact that it had rained throughout the night until the coolness of the humidity-filled air reached my nostrils and rushed into my lungs.

It was just the right cool temperature, and just the right "je ne sais quoi" mixture of damp earth scents to bring rushing to my memory a tender reverie of a glorious time in my life and of a land and people that I would never forget–a time of cheap plastic bonnets and of splashing through the rain.

As I glanced about at the gray, cloud-filled day, I was grateful for the small gift from heaven which helped remind me that there was always something beautiful about each new day—that cloudy days and cleansing rain could not only quench a thirsty earth, but parched souls as well. I felt renewed as I unlocked my car door and felt a few lingering raindrops splash freely on my face. I knew that it was going to be another great day.

"Sing unto the Lord with thanksgiving; sing praise upon the harp unto our God: who covereth the heaven with clouds, who prepareth the rain for the earth" Psalms 147:7, 8.

CHAPTER FIFTEEN

L'Instructeur

The Teacher

It had taken a lot of patient teaching and gentle persuasion to get Madame B to come to church. Several months back, when my companion and I had first started meeting with her in her tiny third story apartment, she had candidly admitted that the only reason she had responded to our brief introduction over the two-way intercom below, buzzing us in, was so that she could brag to her neighbors about having two "Americans girls" visit her. Discussing religion had been the last thing on her mind. After we had climbed the long flights of stairs that wound up to her floor, she somewhat hesitantly opened her own apartment door. Curiously she peeked at us from around the half-opened door and spoke to us as we stood in the corridor. After a few minutes, she timidly invited us in and motioned us to sit down with her in a tiny crowded living room that also doubled as a dining area.

Upon discovering that we were intent on talking to her about religion, Madame B quickly let it be known that she had a general distaste for all organized religions—a distaste which stemmed from her great distrust of her own church. From her point of view, her church was nothing more than a greedy business, with its main goal being that of separating her and her family from their hard-earned money. To Madame B, it seemed that the palm

of the church was constantly turned upward, asking its congregation to give this, and to give that, while giving her and her small family very little—if anything—in return.

Judging from the look of Madame B's very simply furnished, yet immaculate, apartment and her modest, humble attire, it was obvious that money was a scarce commodity in her household. What little money she was able to earn from working as a cleaning lady was used to supplement the meager salary her husband was able to bring home. Even combined, their hard-earned money barely provided them with enough to make ends meet from month to month. In Madame B's reasoning, it was simply ludicrous to think that a large, wealthy church would find it necessary to have to pick her family's pockets of the little resources they struggled like slaves to scrape together—and for what reason other than to build magnificent cathedrals and edifices while the poor and hungry begged in the streets? We assured her in the brief time we were able to spend with her, before she had to scurry off to work that first afternoon we met with her, that our church was not a business, but that it was instead a means for a loving Heavenly Father to bless the lives of His children.

Before ending that initial encounter, we asked Madame B if we could return to talk to her more about a message which we felt would bring her great happiness. She hesitated for a long moment before she responded, obviously weighing in her mind if her fascination with having two American guests with their "drôle" little accents in her home would be worth the risk of having to endure our message about religion. Finally, appearing to succumb to the novelty of potentially acquiring a few foreign friends, she confirmed a time and day in the following week to meet for our next "rendez-vous."

Attempting to teach the discussions to Madame B week after week often felt like driving a car with the handbrake still on as no idea, no principle, no scripture ever went unchallenged. She resisted at times as though her very survival depended on it. But we slowly bumped along, navigating—often at the pace of a very slow escargot—through the myriad of misconceptions and objections about religion that she always raised. Slowly we plodded forward, gaining her trust centimeter by centimeter as the message of the gospel commenced to pry open corner after corner of what had for so long been such a firmly locked heart.

Just as we were beginning to detect some progress with Madame B, my companion received an unexpected transfer to another city, leaving me to face my weekly discussions with Madame B flanked by an adorable—but very sleepy—brand-spanking new missionary fresh from the States. Valiantly, she struggled to simply stay awake during those first few weeks of rather lengthy discussions. Every now and then, she would manage to escape the clutches of new missionary fatigue and flash a supportive smile or a sleepy nod in just the right places, followed by an affirmative "oui" before she lapsed into an eternal battle to keep her eyes from snapping shut. Meanwhile, I continued to spoon-feed the discussions to Madame B, for the most part flying "solo."

The day we finally convinced Madame B to attend a church meeting for the first time felt as miraculous as moving a major mountain range. Not wanting to push our luck by suggesting that she convince her husband—who had always been conspicuously absent on each of our visits—to come, we assured her that we would find a member to drive her to church the next Sunday, since she didn't drive herself and we didn't think she would be too keen on the idea of being transported on the back of one of our bikes.

The next Sunday, my companion and I arrived at church bright and early, anxiously waiting to see if the miracle of Madame B actually attending church was really going to happen. When we finally saw the whites of her wide-opened eyes as she nervously entered the building, my companion and I heaved a collective sigh of relief and then proceeded to greet her, enthusiastically thanking the member who had accompanied her.

After leading her into the chapel, I informed Madame B with a great deal of hesitation that I wouldn't be able to sit with her during the meeting, as I was to be one of the speakers and would be sitting on the stand. Before she could utter a word of objection, I assured her that my companion would be glued to her side and would answer her questions if she had any—never mind the fact that I was fully aware that my companion was still at the point of wondering if the language she had been taught in the MTC was even related to the language they were speaking in the mission field. With that, I left them both sitting on a pew at the front of the church and took my place on the stand.

I was first to speak and gave my talk, catching the sight of Madame B's beaming face from time to time as she smiled up at me from the audience. After I concluded, I took my seat and sat back comfortably in my cushioned chair as the next speaker went to the podium. I didn't recognize the speaker, as he wasn't from our branch, but assumed from his introduction that he was one of the leaders of the district who had been assigned to speak to us that day.

He was not more than a few words into his speech when I had this awful sinking feeling come over me. Apparently the members of the branch had

been struggling with the observation of the law of tithing, and it was this speaker's intention to bring them to a clear understanding of their obligation before the Lord. This talk was by no means a gentle reminder of any sort, one meant to lovingly remind the congregation to pay an honest tithe. Nothing of the sort. It was a fiery, scathing call to repentance.

Timidly, I peeked around the looming body of the speaker in an effort to try and get a glimpse of Madame B. Her face told me the whole story. Her eyes were wide open, her eyebrows were raised in utter astonishment, and her jaw was hanging in a downward, half- open position. The look on my companion's face was not much different. Meekly, I pulled my head back and tried to make myself comfortable, somewhat relieved that I could hide out of sight behind the broad-shouldered body of the speaker for the rest of the talk.

As his podium-pounding talk continued, his chastening tone drew me from my comfortable position, and I once again wondered how Madame B was taking this all in. I felt strangely sick inside as he went from the topic of tithing to extolling the congregation to generously pay the ward budget—a program that was still in implementation at the time. From there he seemed to hit on just about every possible financial obligation or voluntary contribution that was available to members of the church at the time.

It was a scathing talk, to say the very least—one that could have caused full tithe-paying members of the church to squirm a little in their seats. I could only imagine how it had affected our investigator. I got a bit of a clue as I bravely peeked one more time around the speaker as he concluded his remarks. The absolute look of horror on Madame B's ashen face told me everything I needed to know. Slumping down in my chair, I kept my eyes glued on the page of the hymnal throughout the entire closing song until I knew that I could safely shut them and escape any chance of catching Madame B's eye before the closing prayer.

As the meeting concluded and I finally had to make my way out to the foyer where my companion, Madame B and the member driver were waiting, I tried desperately to figure out what I was going to say in the few final seconds I assumed could possibly be the last I would ever speak to Madame B.

As I approached the awaiting trio, I believe I had a tiny glimpse of what it must have felt like for Daniel just before he was to be thrown into the lion's den. Madame B's icy look stared me straight in the eyes—glared might be a better description. When I was finally standing next to her, she shook her upturned hand from side to side as an angry mother would to a disobedient child, which in French body language said, "you deserve to be spanked." Helplessly, I looked at my companion, who had not yet lost her look of bewilderment, then turned to Madame B. "We'll talk to you about this at our next appointment," I feebly assured her.

"You most certainly will," she said. Then, turning on her heel, she exited the building, leaving my companion and me to gape after her.

Completely dejected and frustrated to boot, I headed for the Relief Society room, which just happened to be the closest empty room. Once inside, I snapped the door shut and then broke down into a sniffling, uncontrollable sob while my companion helplessly stared at me. It was as if all the frustration and disappointment for every single investigator who had ever stopped listening to the discussions during my entire mission experience had ganged up on me all at once. I felt so let down and defeated. I couldn't understand why it had been the very act of finally bringing our investigator to church that would serve to unravel all the hard work we had gone through trying to teach her the gospel.

It took awhile to get everything out of my system, while my companion, still so new to the whole experience—and to Madame B—fumbled to console me. When I finally pulled myself together, I wiped my swollen eyes, patted down my splotchy cheeks, gathered up my companion and sneaked out the back door before anyone could see us and start asking questions.

It was an apprehensive week, to say the least, as visions of Madame B's wrath clouded the back of my mind whenever my companion and I worked on preparing the lesson on tithing that we were going to present to her. We prayed that somehow her heart would be softened and that we would know what to say. Finally, the long-awaited day of our rendez-vous with her arrived. Nervously, we knocked on the door of her apartment, not knowing what was awaiting us on the other side. She seemed cordial enough as she greeted us at the door and then motioned for us to sit down. Slowly, we began to make our way through the concepts of the discussion in what was perhaps one of the most meek and humble manners in which the Law of Tithing had ever been presented.

As we got closer and closer to the point in the discussion where we would ask Madame B if she would be willing to live the Law of Tithing, I found myself mentally packing up our discussion chart, offering a final testimony and waving a sad goodbye before she escorted us out the door. Finally, after carefully explaining everything we could about the Law of Tithing, the challenge was delivered. It was followed by a long and almost painful silence.

The Teacher

In the moments that ensued, Madame B taught me a lesson that I would never forget. Quietly and in a tone that was uncharacteristically meek and humble, Madame B, who had been silent and reflective throughout most of the discussion, slowly lifted her head until she looked us both in the eyes.

"At first I was really angry with the both of you, and I wanted to cancel our appointment," she confessed, but then reflectively continued, "but I have been thinking and praying about this all week long."

There wasn't another sound in the room as my companion and I collectively held our breath. She continued, "I feel that I would be willing to commit to the Law of Tithing and pay half of my salary to the church," her humbly sincere voice explained, "but I don't think I can convince my husband to pay half of his."

Her unexpected answer caught me off guard and numbed my senses as I scrambled to make sense of what my ears had just heard. Half her salary! After enthusiastically assuring her that the Lord only asked for ten percent, I quickly glanced around her humble home with only the barest and simplest of necessities, at the same time catching sight of the worn apron that she wore to clean other people's homes hanging on a peg by the door. I felt humbled and reprimanded by my own lack of faith.

I don't remember much more of that discussion, other than the powerful realization that perhaps the greatest teaching that had occurred that day had taken place in my own heart and in my own understanding. Most poignantly, I recognized that while I had been fretting all week long about how we could teach Madame B about the Law of Tithing, she was being humbly taught by the true teacher, the Holy Ghost, who had filled her heart with truth and understanding. It was emblazoned on my heart that day, in a way that I would never forget, that the Holy Ghost is the most powerful teacher; and that it is only through the inspiration and influence of the Holy Ghost—not through the words of man, nor through the prodding and prompting of two little sister missionaries—that the message and understanding of the gospel can enter into our hearts and exercise the tremendous power to change our lives. That day, the greatest "Instructeur" of all had taught us both a lesson I would never forget.

Post Script

I sat in church witnessing the confirmation of the newest member of our ward. It was the type of blessing I had heard countless times throughout the course of my life. As the young girl's father and the circle of other priesthood holders surrounded her and gently placed their hands upon her head, I felt a power in the uttered command "Receive ye the Holy Ghost" that momentarily took my breath away. Silently, I reflected on the magnitude of the great gift that this young girl had just received, a gift to which I had been a quiet witness. It was a gift that might take her a lifetime to truly understand, but a gift I had come to realize was the most precious of all gifts I had ever been given.

My testimony of this sacred gift burned in my heart. With all my soul I knew that this young girl, while still relatively new to this mortal existence, was receiving one of the most powerful gifts available in mortality. With the simple act of her confirmation, she had been given the key to understanding the truth of all things both in heaven and on earth. The same precious gift which had been given to me after my baptism had helped me through each and every day of my life—a gift for which I am daily and eternally grateful.

"And ye shall receive the Holy Ghost, that ye may have all things made manifest" Moses 8:24.

Sister Jackson
Thailand Bangkok Mission
2014

CHAPTER SIXTEEN

La Voix

The Voice

> *"What may appear initially to be a daunting task will be much easier to manage over time as you consistently strive to recognize and follow feelings prompted by the Spirit. Your confidence in the direction you receive from the Holy Ghost will also become stronger. I witness that as you gain experience and success in being guided by the Spirit, your confidence in the impressions you feel can become more certain than your dependence on what you see or hear (Elder Richard G. Scott, "To Acquire Spiritual Guidance,"* Ensign, *Nov. 2009).*

The image in my mind was clear. Try as I might, I couldn't push it away. "Please don't ask me to do this!" I cowardly battled as the impression flashed again across my mind. The tram ride that my companion and I were taking that day was only going to be a short one—just enough to transport us to the center of the big and bustling city we were assigned to as part of our immense teaching area. Having abandoned our bikes in exchange for a more efficient—but less interesting—mode of transportation, we had boarded the tram at a small street level stop that was only a two minute walk from the apartment where we lived on the outskirts of town. Several miles later when the tram would approach the city's busy center, it would dip below the earth's surface into a long dark tunnel before it would deliver us to an "arrêt" not far from a main terminal.

Typically, whenever we used the public transportation system, my companion and I would make an attempt to engage our fellow commuters

in some sort of conversation—that is, if it wasn't during rush hour and we weren't standing packed like sardines in the aisles, holding on for dear life to the strategically placed hand grips, or to each other, in an effort to stay as close to vertical as possible. If we were lucky enough to find a seat and were able to start a conversation with our seat mates, occasionally these friendly conversations would allow us to introduce ourselves and at times, even give us the opportunity to pass out a brochure or two. More often than not, however, most of the other commuters who hopped on the tram would board quickly, glance around for an empty seat, plop themselves down and then immediately retreat from the world around them into a glassy-eyed detached stare out the window for the remainder of the trip. That or hide themselves behind a book or daily newspaper propped up in front of their face, sending out the unmistakable signal that they were desirous of excluding themselves from having to acknowledge—or to converse with—"qui que ce soit."

That particular day, my companion and I were lucky enough to find a comfortable place to sit down near the front of the tram. As all the seats in the car were facing forward—with none of those party-of-four arrangements where you would find yourself in groups that faced each other—we were left with no one we could talk to unless we awkwardly tapped the shoulders of the people in front of us or craned our necks around to talk to the people behind us. Realizing that we had about ten minutes of unexpected repose from our missionary duties, I sat back comfortably in my seat, enjoying a few quiet moments where I could slip into a mindless state of reflection or occasionally glance out the window at the scenery as it passed.

We had not been more than a few minutes into the ride that day, however, when an unsettling image crossed my mind. In it, I saw myself standing boldly in front of the tram with a Book of Mormon in one hand and a handful of brochures in the other, expounding the precepts of the gospel to the captive audience before me. Quickly I pushed the impression of such an unlikely, and quite honestly, frightening scenario out of my mind. I dismissed it as some sort of little guilt trip my mind was taking me on for enjoying the temporary reprise from contacting people on the tram. To add to my discomfort—and perhaps to appease my conscience—I could imagine the disinterested and maybe even hostile looks I might receive in doing such a thing. I wondered if, by actually carrying out such an unusual method of spreading the word, I might even end up getting hauled off by the transportation police for disrupting the quiet commute of a carful of disgruntled travelers. The more I consciously tried not to think about the image that had presented itself to my mind, the more it pressed itself upon me. As my mind continued to play this perplexing little mental game, I began to wonder—more precisely, to worry—if the Spirit were actually trying to tell me something, and if this indeed was something the Lord really wanted me to do.

I was still learning what that little voice sounded like—that quiet, yet distinct voice that would come and impose itself on my mind, sometimes as inconspicuously as a hunch, and impress me with something that I needed to say or to do. Over the course of my mission I had experienced innumerable occasions when it had come to me—often out of the blue like a quiet, fluttering butterfly—whispering this, or prompting that, so often encouraging me to do or to understand things that I couldn't possibly have thought of or understood on my own. Powerfully, I had seen the undeniable fruit that stemmed from listening to and following that voice; it had come as a repeated and unmistakable witness throughout my mission. It was, nevertheless, a voice I was still coming to know—and more importantly, to trust at a deeper and more profound level. But this time I felt so terribly weak—and so very mortal.

"Please don't make me do this," I repeated over in my mind as the tram entered the tunnel and began its final descent toward the station.

We had only been in the belly of the tunnel a minute or two when suddenly the tram lurched to a dead stop, and the cabin became dark except for a small yellowish emergency light that dimly lit the entrance. Suddenly, all around me, daily papers were folded together and open books were snapped closed as people who had previously been silently detached from each other began conversing across aisles. Questioningly, they looked around the cabin of the tram, searching for answers.

"What do you think the problem is?" someone could be heard to ask. "How long do you think it will take to fix it?" others queried. The lady behind us suggested that maybe we should get out and walk along the dark track until we got to the next station, which was quickly dismissed by someone sitting nearby as being "trop dangereux."

Craning our necks, we turned our heads to see the lady behind us who had made this suggestion and struck up a conversation. The young girl who was seated beside her immediately became curious as to where we were from and what two American girls were doing in her city so far away from home. After several more minutes of introduction and explanation, we heard the man in front of us somewhat jokingly ask, "Does anyone have a good history book I could read?"

The Voice

With that, we tapped him on the shoulder and informed him that as a matter of fact, we just so happened to have a very good history book with us that he could read. We explained that it was the history of the ancient inhabitants of the American continent. What ensued was a brief introduction to and discussion of the Book of Mormon, which I pulled from my purse and eventually gave him, along with an invitation to hear more. Overhearing our conversation, several other people around us began to curiously listen in. In the next few minutes, before the lights to the tram fluttered back on and we began to slowly advance towards the next station, we had managed to give away some additional brochures, give a brief introduction to the Book of Mormon and hand out the address of the church to several people on the tram.

I left that tram feeling humbled and duly chastened. It wasn't lost on me that I had almost failed to deliver a message to one of Heavenly Father's children who was on that tram—a message which was so important to Him that He had brought a tram to a screeching halt in that underground tunnel in order for it to be delivered. Meekly grateful for the forgiveness that had been extended in giving me that second chance, I covenanted to better listen and to more courageously follow those heaven-sent promptings from that moment on.

Post Script

It hadn't been more than a few months since I had returned home from my mission. A few friends, including one of my beloved MTC companions, had talked me into rooming together in an apartment located just a few miles from the college we were attending. One evening, I left my upstairs room and headed down the stairs; I was mid-step, ready to take the next step down into the living room, when the quiet but clearly distinct impression came to me, "Go talk to your roommate. She needs you."

For a split-second I found myself wavering on what I should do, knowing full well that while a dear friend, my roommate was also a very private person who rarely opened up or talked about things that might be troubling her. Yet the voice was clear and I recognized it from the many times it had come to me on my mission.

When my foot reached the landing of the next step, I immediately did an about face and headed back up the stairs towards my roommate's room. Hesitantly, I stopped by the door before quietly knocking, not knowing in advance what would greet me or what I was going to say, but trusting that the same voice that had led me there would also give me the words to speak. An almost imperceptible voice responded to my quiet rap on the door.

"Who is it?" the voice inquired.

Somewhat apologetically, I cracked open the door and peeked my head in. On the bed, curled up in a ball, was my roommate, her eyes swollen with tears that had streamed down her face and dampened her pillow. I had never seen her like that in all the time I had known her. To me, she had always appeared so on top of things; she had seemed to have the world by the tail. Half expecting her to embarrassedly turn away and attempt to act like everything was okay, I simply asked, "Do you need to talk?"

With that she turned to look up at me where I was standing in the doorway and whispered, "I knew you would come."

We talked about what was on her mind and in her heart well into the early hours of the morning—just long enough for a dearly beloved and watched-over daughter of God to dry up her tears and gently fall back to sleep.

I left her room that night very sleepy, but eternally grateful

The Voice

for the countless opportunities I had been given during my mission to truly learn to recognize and to trust enough to follow that priceless voice from heaven.

"Yea, behold, I will tell you in your mind and in your heart, by the Holy Ghost, which shall come upon you and which shall dwell in your heart" Doctrine and Covenants 8:2.

Sister Schmuhl
Brussels Belgium Mission
Christmas Day, 1993

CHAPTER SEVENTEEN
Les Fêtes
The Holidays

{ *"Crisis or transition of any kind reminds us of what matters most. In the routine of life, we often take our families...for granted. But in times of danger and need and change, there is no question that what we care about most is our families! . . . Create meaningful family bonds. . . . This can be done through family traditions for birthdays, for holidays, for dinnertime, and for Sundays"* (M. Russell Ballard, *"What Matters Most Is What Lasts Longest,"* October 2005 General Conference). }

t was hard to believe that it had been a whole year since I had first stepped off the plane to begin the foreign part of my mission—and that I was now headed into my second round of the holiday season as a missionary. I could remember the details of the very first series of holidays I had celebrated as if they had happened yesterday.

Just before my first Christmas in the mission field, my companion and I sped through a dark and sleepy town one night en route to our apartment. Suddenly, having spotted something in the road, I pulled hard on the brakes of my bike then braced to keep my balance as my two screeching tires skidded to a sudden halt against the hard asphalt. Gripping the handlebars, I straddled the frame of my bike and slowly walked it backwards until I arrived at the object lying at the side of the road that had caught my attention. Holding my bike in one hand, I reached down with the other and picked up what appeared to be a single branch of a live evergreen tree or "sapin" which had somehow detached itself from a Christmas tree on its way to someone's home.

Upon hearing the screech of my brakes, my companion circled her bike back to find me ecstatically examining the find I held in my hands. Her puzzled expression as she approached where I was standing—still straddling my bike—made it perfectly clear that she didn't understand in the least degree the value of my treasure nor the expediency of my hasty and somewhat reckless stop.

As it was, we were already going to be quite late arriving back at our apartment that night. The weekly English class we had been teaching in the tiny town next to where we lived had gone a little bit over that evening, making it difficult—if not impossible—for us to arrive home before our nightly curfew, even though we had been pedaling through the dark and empty streets of town at breakneck speed. We had been making great time until I had suddenly interrupted our hasty return home with my unexplainable—at least in the eyes of my companion—stop at the side of the road.

When she circled back to see what had made me stop, I unsuccessfully tried to convince her that what I held in my hands was our future apartment Christmas tree. Immediately aware that she somehow didn't share my same enthusiasm for the scrawny bough which was delicately cradled in my arms, I felt very much like a small child holding a stray puppy in front of a leery mom as I attempted to persuade her that it was a good idea to let me take it home.

Whether or not it was a good idea, my companion watched me curiously, even offering a few suggestions from time to time as I attempted to figure out exactly how I was going to transport the awkwardly shaped potential Christmas tree back to our apartment on my bike—something I hadn't given a minute's thought to before I had decided to give it a home. I was confident however, that I could figure out a way to do it. After all, it had only taken a few P-days of carrying a week's worth of laundry on the front fender of my bike and a week's worth of groceries on the back for me to learn that with a few strategically placed bungee straps and a little bit of balance, it was possible to carry just about anything on a bike.

While visions of sugar plums danced merrily through my head, I carefully proceeded to strap my early Christmas gift to the rack of my bike, making sure not to break any of its precious few branches in the process. I then hopped on my bike with my little bundle and headed for home. Which didn't work at all. The gangly limb protruded so precariously off the back of the bike that I could scarcely go a half a block or so before the wind would catch it and whip it off to one side where it would threaten to become entangled in the spokes. After a few false starts and stops, I eventually gave up on the bungee idea and decided to just tuck it under my arm, holding on to it firmly in one hand while I single-handedly steered and braked my bike with the other. Gingerly, I nursed my hard earned Christmas cheer for the next several miles until we finally arrived at our apartment.

The next evening, I worked laboriously to cut and then to reposition some of the small branches jutting off the bigger branch in an effort to make our branch look more like a tree. Carefully I wired the amputated branches into their new and lofty positions. Finally joining in the Christmas spirit, my companion hung her only surviving ornament from her previous Christmas in the field on what was looking remarkably like our very own "Charlie Brown" Christmas tree. We finished off the decorations with some elaborately cut-out snowflakes and paper chains before we placed a three-tiered paper nativity scene in front of it on the table where it humbly brightened our small apartment and quietly reminded us of the true reason for the upcoming season. It was the best we could do in our circumstances, but at least it was something, and for the time being, it was exactly enough for my first missionary Christmas.

At the time of that first memorable Christmas celebration, I had only been in France for a total of three short weeks, but was already heading into my third holiday in the field. My first one had been Thanksgiving, which had taken place just one day after my arrival as a brand-spanking new mission-ary. It seemed that I had just barely unpacked my bags and stepped into my apartment as the newest greenie in town, when my sleepy ears learned that we would be spending the next day celebrating Thanksgiving with the Elders in our district—and that they would be cooking. Upon waking up on that next bright—and far too early—morning and being informed that we would be wearing our "p-days" to our Thanksgiving celebration, I quickly discov-ered that I had come totally unprepared with any sort of casual clothing that could actually be worn in public. Facing my first "what-to-wear" missionary dilemma, my resourceful companion kindly helped me find something ap-propriate from the box of "left behind" clothing that past sisters had donated to the cause in an effort to empty out their suitcases for the long flight home.

Decked out in my new "used" duds, I made my way to the church where we were meeting the Elders for our feast of gratitude, blearily pedaling through unfamiliar streets and neighborhoods. Everywhere, I saw French people going about their business as usual. It was amazing to realize that an entire country of people had absolutely no desire to celebrate—with lavish meals and extensive family gatherings—the fact that long ago American pilgrims and Native American Indians had sat down and shared a peaceable meal together.

I didn't know what to expect when we arrived at the church house and made our way to the small kitchen where I was to meet the Elders who had been responsible for "creating" our Thanksgiving feast. As a matter of fact, there was no possible way I could have anticipated what actually greeted me. I was still so fresh from the MTC that I could almost smell the Thanksgiving dinner I knew was being prepared by the cooks for the missionaries who would be spending the holiday there. I felt a slight pang of homesickness as I imagined where my family would be and what they would be doing. I had always cherished spending special time together with my large, noisy family when we gathered to celebrate the holidays. Clusters of adults would pass hours upon hours just chatting, playing games and laughing together about favorite family stories while gangs of cousins noisily played their hearts out, gleefully running from room to room.

I wasn't immediately sure that I recognized the unique "mélange" of odors that accosted my senses as we entered the kitchen and caught sight of the small cluster of Elders who were grouped around the stove busily making last minute preparations. As we entered, they eagerly looked up at us like little boys waiting for their parents to open presents they had spent days hand-making for them. Straightening up, they wiped their hands off on their make-shift aprons and then extended a friendly, arm's length hand shake and "bienvenue" to the new sister before inviting us to take a seat at a small table they had set.

Although it was readily apparent that the Elders' hearts and souls had been fully invested in the meal preparation, it didn't take more than a few hesitant bites—when we finally began to eat some forty-five minutes later—to discover that their desire to produce a feast like their mom's homemade cooking had not been accompanied by a mastery of finer culinary skills.

An immediate apology only seconds after the prayer had been given for having frozen turkey patties instead of "real" turkey, should have prepared us for what was to come, but it didn't. After all, it had sounded like a perfectly acceptable substitution given that fact that the French had no real reason to have an abundant supply of twenty pound-plus birds gracing their stores at that time of year. The piece of meat that eventually made it to our plates, however, while close to being burnt to a crisp on the outside, had remained nevertheless quite pink—and cold—on the inside.

It didn't help matters much that the gravy—which was now only luke-warm because it had been sitting on the table for so long while the Elders had finished preparing the rest of the meal—looked like some kind of cloudy set-up gelatin dotted with unidentifiable lumps and textures. Poured over the paste-like mashed potatoes that had been slapped generously on our plates, this gravy became hard to distinguish from potatoes themselves as they both were so full of lumps.

Perhaps too tired and too hungry for it to make any difference, I bravely attempted to politely eat what I could, trying hard not to think about what I was truly eating. All went relatively well until it came to the dressing. Immediately noticing on first contact with our tongues that the dressing seemed to be very heavily seasoned—a gross understatement at best—my companion curiously asked what recipe the Elders had used to make it. Proudly, one of them explained that they'd used a recipe his mother had sent him.

"Only the recipe called for quite a lot more bread than we had," he candidly admitted. Then continuing on, he explained, "So we just followed the recipe as it was written, and used the one 'baguette' we did have."

"We didn't think it would make that much difference," his companion chimed in.

My taste buds, which were fighting to keep the dressing going down my throat in the right direction, begged to differ.

Of course, it was an understandable error for two barely wet-behind-the-ears but well-intentioned young chefs. I could have, nevertheless, gone all day—and perhaps all of my life—without hearing the next details of their Thanksgiving cooking adventure.

"We didn't have a bowl in the apartment that was big enough to mix the dressing in," they hesitantly admitted, "so we cleaned out the bathtub and made it in there."

I never found out if they were telling the truth or just trying to gross out the new sister missionary. All I know is that it had worked. Really well. Suddenly I was full—and done with my first missionary Thanksgiving dinner. I made a mental note: the next Thanksgiving, my companion and I would be responsible for making the Thanksgiving dinner.

My second holiday celebration that first year had come as a bit of surprise to me one day as my companion and I were street contacting "en ville." I couldn't

The Holidays

help but notice the tall, skinny saintly figure who paraded up and down the "trottoir" in a long red robe with a tall ornate hat perched ceremoniously on his head. In one hand he carried what appeared to be a tall shepherd's crook. He was accompanied by a hunched-over elf as well as a persistent photographer who followed him around. The photographer repetitively tried—without the least bit of success—to convince my companion to have us pose for an instant souvenir photo with the parading duo "to take back with us to America" —for a hefty price, of course. Once safely past the photographer's grasp, I questioned my companion as to who the skinny Santa Claus-like figure was. I learned that he was Saint Nicolas, the patron saint of little school children and the chief figure in a regionally celebrated "fête" that would be observed on December 6, known as the "Fête de Saint Nicolas."

The night of the 5th of December, I enjoyed my first look at that particular celebration as we participated in "une petite soirée" with the enthusiastic members of the Branch who sent us home at the end of the night with sacks, instead of shoes—as is the tradition—bursting full of "les fruits et noix."

My third holiday, after only a matter of weeks in France, was Noël, which had been shaping up to be a very meager celebration—at least for me—until I had spied our lowly "Christmas tree" lying by the side of the road. I had tried not to notice that the recent deluge of cards, letters and packages in our mailbox were always addressed either to my companion or to some other sister missionary who had been transferred to another city.

To put it lightly, I was starving as far as communication from home went. Only one solitary letter had appeared in our mailbox with my name scrawled on it since I had arrived and that was from the mission home simply to inform me that my parents had gotten word that I had arrived safely in France. I hadn't even received my first check that was supposed to cover my initial rent and expenses. To make matters worse, my companion hadn't received her check either. As a result, we found out what it really felt like to be without purse or script and poorer than church mice as the holidays rolled around.

Nevertheless, desiring to spread a little Christmas cheer to the people we were teaching—and to the saintly members who somehow knew we were scraping to get by and had left some much needed bags of groceries and goodies at our doorstep—we gathered together the empty pop bottles that had been collecting under our sink and cashed them in for a few "francs" at a local store. With the meager funds we were able to come up with, we bought a few materials to make the "cartes de Noël" we had decided to hand out. With the willing help of a couple of girls from the Branch, we reverted back to school-aged pastimes and spent one night giggling and dipping the cut off edge of a potato—which had been carved with a little Christmas scene—into ink and then onto the paper we had bought to make our cards.

The night before Christmas, having been invited to enjoy an official "Réveillon"—or a large, sumptuous meal of never-ending courses—with a member family, I found myself facing my very own, generously heaping plate of fresh oysters to begin the meal. I had spent an entire lifetime dodging oysters. My mom and dad loved them and had regularly served them up in my dad's favorite recipe of oyster stew, always saving a few fresh ones to be eaten on the side. I was an expert at fishing the oysters out of my stew and sending them back to the pot. In all my life, I had seen to it that they had never once made it past my lips. Now faced with this graciously offered delicacy, I knew that I could no longer dodge them without offending our hosts. Bravely, I forced them to slimily slither, one by one, down my throat until they had

Sister Dominault and Sister Young with the Kusseling family where I celebrated my first Christmas Eve. The Kusseling's worked with us and would often surprise us with bags of food and goodies left at our apartment door.

The Holidays

all safely landed in the pit of my stomach, not once allowing myself to even consider how close to actually being alive they had probably been. I took a deep breath when I had successfully finished the task, finding some solace in knowing that I would have made my dad proud.

The rest of the meal, which literally lasted for several hours, was a wonderful array of deliciously flavored and beautifully presented "plat" after "plat." Quickly I learned why the French were so renowned for their food. However, as each new plate was brought out, I found myself seriously regretting the space those oysters were taking up in my stomach as I endeavored to find room for it all.

My LTM companion, Sister O'Brien finds the porcelain king while celebrating the "Fête des Rois" a holiday in January that commemorates the arrival of the three Wisemen. Brussels Belgium Mission, 1976.

Little clay figurines known as "Santons" are an important part of the French "crèche" or nativity scene. They represent the people of the village as they come to see the Christ child.

At Christmas time, the windows of the "pâtisseries" or pasty shops are overflowing with chocolate representations of "Père Noël."

The Holidays

The special evening concluded with a broadcast of a Tabernacle Choir Christmas presentation which was being aired over a German television station. My heart leaped at the thought of how relatively close those cameras were to "chez moi" when an aerial view of Temple Square flashed on the screen. I was certain that the camera man would point his camera just a little further south and send me back images of my home and of my family, but that was not to be. Still, my heart went temporarily home for the holidays.

My companion and I left our special night-before-Christmas celebration, basking in the warmth and the love of this wonderful family who had shared with us the beautiful Christmas spirit. Along with all that they had done, they had thoughtfully sent us home with a brightly wrapped gift to share between us. Since I hadn't received anything from home—and therefore didn't have a single thing to open after we read the Christmas story on Christmas morning—my companion insisted that I open the gift we had received the night before. Carefully I peeled back the festive layers of wrapping paper as slowly as I could, making the moment last as long as possible.

"Oh boy, snails!" I choked out as enthusiastically as humanly possible—not wanting to sound ungrateful after catching my first peek of one of those French delicacies staring back at me from the cover of the box I had just unwrapped so carefully. My mind raced ahead of me trying to figure out what on earth I would possibly do with so many "escargots."

As I worked to open the resistant lid of the large box my companion, looking at first almost apologetic, watched as the lid finally came off and then appeared puzzled when my face broke into a hard-to-miss expression of relief.

"They're chocolates in the shape of snails!" I announced, clearly relieved.

Four deliciously sumptuous snails later, my companion and I concluded that we had just consumed what might have been the best snails ever, and we reveled in the wonder of truly fine French chocolate and a truly memorable first Christmas in the field.

Nearly a year later, I fulfilled the promise I had made to myself after having endured that Elder-sponsored Thanksgiving meal my first day in the field. Reflectively, I thought back on those preliminary days as a missionary as I stirred the smoother-than-silk gravy, and peeked in at the baking pies. I could hear the thump of the volleyball in the cultural hall as the Elders enthusiastically kept themselves busy—and out of the kitchen—until it was time to eat.

I uncovered the turkey to check it one more time as the tempting aroma of a well roasted—but not too done—Belgian turkey escaped and reached my senses. With the familiar scents of a beloved family holiday all around me, my mind and heart temporarily escaped to a place far off. To a place where I could imagine exactly what those people who I loved with all my heart, and to whom I belonged, had done for that very special day, and just where they had gathered to chat and laugh. In that moment, I was comforted in knowing that no matter how many miles separated me from my family and my loved ones, my heart would always know how to find its way home for the holidays.

Post Script

Our little corner of the inclining hill was filling up quickly as family members and friends claimed a blanket to prepare to watch the city's annual 4th of July fireworks display together. We didn't have to tell anyone where to find us; they just always knew. We had been at the same place, and in fact, had enjoyed the same 4th of July routine all day long from parade to picnic for practically as long as I could remember.

There was something safe and unifying about doing the same things year after year, things that belonged to just you and your family—shared traditions that bonded you to each other as a unique entity and reinforced the feeling that you belonged together. Each holiday and family event created cherished time together filled with people and places you could send your heart home to whenever you might find yourself far away from home, just as I did for those two holiday seasons as a missionary.

"And the same sociality which exists among us here will exist among us there, only it will be coupled with eternal glory" Doctrine and Covenants 130:2

Sister Dominault and my companion, Sister
Nelson, waiting for the tram that will
take Sister Dominault to the Mission Home to
officially end her mission.

CHAPTER EIGHTEEN

Son Amour

His Love

> "I testify that the tender mercies of the Lord are real and that they do not occur randomly or merely by coincidence. Often, the Lord's timing of his tender mercies helps us to both discern and acknowledge them. . . . The Lord's tender mercies are the very personal and individualized blessings, strength, protection, assurances, guidance, loving-kindnesses, consolation, support, and spiritual gifts which we receive from and because of and through the Lord Jesus Christ. . . . Faithfulness, obedience and humility invite tender mercies into our lives, and it is often the Lord's timing that enables us to recognize and treasure these important blessings. . . . I testify that the tender mercies of the Lord are available to all of us and that the Redeemer of Israel is eager to bestow such gifts upon us. . . . Each of us can have eyes to see clearly and ears to hear distinctly the tender mercies of the Lord as they strengthen and assist us in these latter days" (David A. Bednar, "The Tender Mercies of the Lord," April 2005 General Conference).

"What are you doing here?" I asked in bewildered astonishment as my companion and I pushed open the door to our apartment and caught sight of my former companion, Sister Dominault. She shyly approached us. Had my jaw been able to drop any lower I'm sure there would have been some kind of audible thud as it hit the floor, so great was my surprise at seeing her standing there before us in our apartment like some kind of apparition. My muddled mind scrambled desperately to try and make some sense of this strangely unexpected guest. After all, it had only been a few hours earlier that we had waved a tearful goodbye to her at the Mission Home before she was to be driven to the train that would eventually deliver her to her home in northern France, thus bringing her mission experience to an end.

It had been a tender farewell to a companion who had become like a sister to me in every sense of the word. As we had parted, a prevailing sense of sadness had accompanied this final goodbye. It was hard to fathom that her mission had passed so quickly. Adding to the tenderness of the moment had been the very real possibility that it just might be a very long time before we would ever see each other again—if ever—as we most likely would be living the majority of our lives in two different countries. It was difficult to imagine what life after a mission would be like for Sister Dominault. Her whole life would change in a matter of hours; after almost sixteen months of being a missionary myself, it felt as if that was the only life I could seem to remember.

Sister Dominault had been assigned to be my second companion, after I had served five months with my first companion. Initially, when I had learned that I would be receiving a French sister as my new companion—and one who spoke very little English at that—I was in all honesty, terrified. Although my French had been coming along—slowly but surely—my language ability was still very much a work in progress. The thought of being in a perpetual state of only semi-understanding what was being said as well as only half-communicating what I really wanted to say—twenty-four seven—caused the butterflies that had been forming in my stomach to begin to fly out of formation. Besides that, I knew my poor little tired brain would dearly miss the luxury of coming home each and every night finally able to freely communicate whatever I wanted to say without first having to plan the whole thing out in my head in advance. To make matters worse, I was keenly aware that my "dans l'appartement" French vocabulary was severely lacking; I feared that if the subject of the conversation turned to much more than what was contained in the discussions or in passages of scripture, I knew I could be in trouble.

During the long hours after having said good-bye to my first companion and while waiting alone in my apartment for the Elders to escort me to the train station in order to meet and greet my new one, I stared at the large map of our tracting area pinned to the wall of my apartment. As I did, the overwhelming thought occurred to me that I would now be the one who would have to actually lead the companionship around our "grand quartier."

Even though I had spent many a day pedaling my bike through our huge tracting area and around our beautiful city, I still had somehow managed to remain about a half block behind my speeding companion despite my best efforts to close the gap. As a result of having perpetually been in the position of bringing-up-the-rear, I had never really had the responsibility of finding where we were going completely on my own. Basically, all I had needed to do was to follow. Of course my vantage point in the rear had had its advantages: I could pedal, unencumbered, letting my mind wander from time to time while I took in the scenery as it whizzed by or I reflected on the more weighty matters of the kingdom. I had learned from that rear-guard position that as long as I kept one eye on my companion's bobbing head, I could get where I needed to go without getting lost. Most of the time. But all that would change with this new transfer. Now, at least for the first little while, I would have to pay attention as I would ride in the number one position and at least have to be able to appear to know where we were going—without making it too apparent that most of the time I really didn't.

Added to those concerns was the fact that I would have to bring my new companion up to speed on everyone we were teaching—or at least trying to teach. Figuring out how to summarize five months of searching, teaching, encouraging, challenging, and not giving up on what amounted to be about twenty-five different families—all of whom were in different stages of their progression toward eternity—was a daunting task, even in one's own language. I had to admit that I was suddenly quite grateful for the sometimes tedious records my companion had been so diligent at making sure we had kept up to date. Unfortunately, all our records had been kept in English, which I hoped somehow to be able to explain to my new companion. Either that, or gain quick access to a Urim and Thummin.

I soon learned that all my concerns, and butterflies, had been wasted worries. They quickly disappeared the moment Sister Dominault stepped off the train. She was gracious, loving and charming. After not more than a few minutes in our apartment and almost before we had even set her bags down, my new companion suggested beginning our time together with a companion prayer. The depth of her spirituality and her great love for the Lord were quickly evident as she prayed in her eloquent French for our companionship. She prayed that we would be guided by the Spirit and that we would be instruments in conveying the love of our Father in Heaven to others. My heart was especially moved by her prayer for me; she prayed that the language

His Love

would continue to come quickly, and I that I would be blessed with the ability to express those things that were in my heart. The sweet spirit that began our companionship and filled our apartment that day continued to bless our companionship for the entire time we served together. It would be a time, and a friendship, I would long remember and which would impact the manner in which I served the rest of my mission, as well as my life.

Despite the immediate bond we had felt, getting used to the language barrier did at times provide us with more than a few awkward moments—like the time I'd been busy pouring my heart and soul into preparing a special lesson for an investigator. Casually, Sister Dominault had looked up from what she was doing and commented in a sweet tone—a tone that seemed to betray the uncharacteristically critical message she had then delivered in telling me that I must have "une grosse tête." Stunned at having been so candidly informed that I had a "big head" by my normally kind and gentle companion, I'd tried bravely to hide the hurt expression that I'm sure must have registered—at least temporarily—on my face. Chastised and duly humbled, I'd meekly returned to preparing my lesson, trying all the while to not give off such a haughty impression as the one I must have given.

It only took half a mission, and a bazillion similar miscommunications later, to discover that the idiomatic expression "avoir une grosse tête" (thus named "idiomatic" because you feel like an idiot when you discover what the expression really means) actually meant "to be knowledgeable." A few months past due, I graciously thanked Sister Dominault for the kind compliment she had paid me—only this time doing so with my much improved French.

Despite, and maybe even in part due to, all the language gaffs and the laughs we suffered through in our effort to communicate with each other, I began to learn, in a very real way, that there exists a powerful spirit-to-spirit communication—a communication that often gets ignored when we have the luxury of words to communicate our thoughts and feelings. I relied heavily on that communication during the preliminary months of my mission until my language skills caught up with my tongue. I still wonder how much more effective communication would be, on the whole, if we could somehow train ourselves to listen to that spiritual communication in tandem with the spoken word.

Teaching with Sister Dominault was an exhilarating and insightful experience. The Spirit was so very present and edifying in those lessons that I always left them feeling uplifted and renewed. Somehow we seemed to be of one heart and of one mind, capable of teaching in a continuous stream, with one picking up where the other one left off, finding a little part of Zion in our missionary team.

As it seems it is with all good things, those wonderfully edifying teaching moments with Sister Dominault ended far too soon; after only one month into our companionship, I received notice that I would be transferring to a new city on the other side of France. It brought to a close a brief but wonderful part of my mission—an experience that I would always look back on and which would set a standard for the rest of my mission.

Throughout the ensuing months, as both of our missions progressed along with our ability to communicate in each other's language, I often found myself yearning to be able to enjoy the experience of teaching, just one more time, with Sister Dominault before our missions ended. It was a tiny hope and desire that I kept tucked secretly in my heart my entire mission. As I had watched the remaining months in her mission slowly trickle down to the last day and then had waved a final goodbye as we had left her at the Mission Home, I finally had had to resign myself to the fact that it just would never happen.

Yet there she was before me, standing mystifyingly present in my apartment when she was supposed to be on her way home. I was at a loss to know what to think.

"There was an unexpected train strike tonight," she informed us, as I struggled to return my gaping jaw to its proper position. While strikes in France were nothing surprising and were in fact, practically as normal as breathing to the French, they generally were just annoying. They took on a very personal nature to us, however, when they had anything to do with the disruption of the mail delivery service. Then, news of a strike became as serious an event to missionaries as cutting off oxygen or taking away food for a day, or a week, or however long it took to settle whatever it was that had caused the strike in the first place. News of this strike, though—and the perfect timing of it—was for me like receiving a little gift from heaven.

Before I even had time or the presence of mind to formulate the question as to how my former companion had gotten past a locked door in order to appear like a spirit from another world in our apartment, she answered it for me. The Mission President, upon learning that Sister Dominault would not be able to leave for home until the next morning, had suggested that she arrange to stay with us for the night. Conveniently, the lady who lived in the apartment at the bottom of the stairs was also a member of the church and just so happened to have a key to our apartment.

His Love

Immediately upon hearing such glad tidings, my mind began to buzz with plans of how we would prepare for Sister Dominault's overnight stay. Fortunately, true to her missionary-to-the-very-end spirit, she interrupted my thoughts by curiously inquiring, "Do you happen to have any more appointments that I could go on with you tonight?"

"Yes! Oui! Yes!" My bumbling bilingual tongue couldn't make the answer tumble out of my mouth fast enough as I immediately grasped the significance of what she was asking. In the bewilderment of finding my former companion in my apartment, I had completely forgotten that we even had another appointment that night. As a matter of fact, we had actually already been "en route" to that very appointment—having gone straight from another one we had just finished—when about half way there I had felt impressed to turn around and get some additional materials from our apartment.

It was almost incomprehensible to believe that because of that little detour, as well the perfect lining up of so many other unlikely events, the one little desire I had tucked away in my heart for most of my mission was just about to be fulfilled: I couldn't believe I was going to have one more chance to teach with Sister Dominault!

It didn't take much to convince my greener-than-green companion to hand the main teaching part of that lesson over to Sister Dominault and me that night, and she instead sat supportively by, interjecting an occasional word here or there while she turned the pages of the flip chart.

Teaching with Sister Dominault was just as I had remembered. The moment was made even sweeter by the fact that we had both grown and had learned a lot more about how to be missionaries since those preliminary days of teaching together. Needless to say, my grateful heart was full to bursting as we returned home that evening and I reflected on the wonder of all that had taken place.

Not long after having put Sister Dominault to bed that night after chatting together just about as long as we legally could as missionaries—or maybe even a teeny bit longer—I knelt beside my bed to say my prayers, not knowing where to start. The tears started to roll freely down my cheeks long before I found the words to express all that I was feeling. After a multitude of heartfelt "merci's," I simply remained on my knees with my head bowed for a long time, bathing in the wonder of the moment and too overcome by the realization of my Savior's love for me to end my prayer.

As I contemplated the fact that what had just happened was, in all reality, just a tiny little thing in the grand scheme of things, that understanding made it somehow all the more significant. It was certainly nothing earth-shattering or anything bearing eternal significance, but I felt that the seeming insignificance of the act made it so much more profoundly significant to me. It was an understanding that somehow in the middle of His truly important business of running a universe, a loving Savior had cared enough about a little sister missionary with a tiny hidden desire—had cared about me—that He had taken the time to look deep into my heart and see to it that I could teach with my beloved companion once again before she ended her mission. It was in that understanding that I felt His love as I had never felt it before. I stayed on my knees that night for a long time, humbled and amazed at the thought.

Though it was truly impossible for me to comprehend a love so personal and so encompassing, I felt engulfed by it as I finished my prayers and crawled into bed that night, tucking in with me a deeper understanding of God's love that would serve to carry me through hard times to come.

I learned that night that sometimes the seemingly small things in life—the small prayers that are answered, the small tender mercies that are accorded us—are, in all actuality, the really big things.

Post Script

Our hearts were tender as our small group of family members entered the temple chapel the afternoon after having just rendered one final act of service to our beloved father. Just moments before, we had tearfully left the mortuary where our father's viewing was to be held later on that evening. We'd been given the special privilege of helping to dress him in the temple clothes he would be buried in the next day and we had gathered at the mortuary to put those sacred robes on him before bidding a final "adieu" and then leaving to attend a temple session together. Before leaving the mortuary, I couldn't help but add, "See you at the temple, Dad."

His Love

As my family quietly entered the temple chapel, the sweet tones of the organ reverently filled the room with the hymn "Abide with me." Collectively, we caught our breath as the music reached our ears, and looks of wonder passed from one family member to another. Through reading in our father's journal shortly after his passing, we had discovered that this particular hymn held a special meaning for him and thus we'd prepared to sing it as a family at his funeral the next day. Our hearts were tender as we reverently took our seats and reflectively listened to the rest of the song.

Immediately after the sacred tones of that hymn had finished, the organist quietly transitioned into the next hymn; "I Need Thee Every Hour." Again, bewildered glances were exchanged furtively among us as the tune to another of our father's favorite hymns tenderly registered in our heart. It seemed so coincidental, as this too was one of the other songs that we had chosen to be a part of his funeral services. Moments later, when the third hymn, "Be Still My Soul," quietly filled that hallowed room, we were reduced to tenderly grateful tears. Just as with the other two hymns, that hymn was a special one to my father and was also going to be included as a special number at his funeral.

We left the temple that day overcome and forever moved by the celestially-aided alignment of those inspired hymns and by the tender mercy of the Lord that had been extended to our grieving family that day. Through that small, but immensely personal heavenly gesture, we knew beyond a doubt that He loved us—beyond degree—and that our beloved father was safe in His tender care.

"I am encircled about eternally in the arms of his love" 2 Nephi 1:15.

CHAPTER NINETEEN
Le Prix
The Price

> *"All [the Lord] asks is that you give your best effort and your whole heart. Do it cheerfully and with the prayer of faith. The Father and His Beloved Son will send the Holy Ghost as your companion to guide you. Your efforts will be magnified in the lives of the people you serve. And when you look back on what may now seem trying times of service and sacrifice, the sacrifice will have become a blessing, and you will know that you have seen the arm of God lifting those you served for Him, and lifting you" (Elder Henry B. Eyring, "Rise to Your Call," Ensign, Oct. 2002).*

Soeur, I think you fell asleep again saying your prayers," I whispered, gently tapping the shoulder of the fresh-from-the-States missionary. She was kneeling once again—her head motionlessly collapsed on her folded arms—by the side of the living room couch in petrified prayer position. It was the fourth night in a row I had woken up at the wee hour of 2:00 AM only to find her in exactly the same position we had left her in hours ago when the other three of us sharing the apartment had finished our own prayers, said good-night for the evening and then climbed into our beds.

I was in what was the third and final city of my mission. It was the first time I had been assigned to an area which my companion and I were not the only sister missionaries serving in what at times had seemed like a radius of a hundred miles or more. In just one transfer my mission world went from one set of sisters per city to three sets, making the magic number a total of six "soeurs" serving together in the same city—with four of us living in the same apartment. It was like living in sister heaven.

What made it even better was that a sister in the other companionship living in my apartment was one of my very own MTC companions. Somehow, it seemed only fitting that we were able to close the final chapter of our mission experiences rejoicing together over conversions rather than crying over verb conjugations, as we had in the beginning. As an added bonus, both of us had been given our very own most-of-the-time sleepy, but always enthusiastic "bleues" to train—and occasionally awaken from their dozing positions.

The last few months of my mission had sped along as though they were careening through the hour glass of time. Finally, everything seemed to be clicking on all four cylinders with the blessings of a harvest—after a long season of thrusting in the sickle—coming in fast and furiously in every direction. I couldn't imagine any life other than that of being a missionary and serving the Lord twenty-four-seven. I wanted to hang on to every second, to every experience.

The first night that I noticed my MTC companion's newbie still on her knees at 2:00 AM, I simply marveled at what an incredibly long and meaningful evening prayer she was having before I sleepily rolled over and fell back to sleep. However, when I awoke a little while later to the distinctive breathing of someone who was obviously sound asleep, I threw back my covers and quietly tip-toed from my bed so as not to disrupt the other two missionaries in the room, and rescued the sleeping—and consequentially very cold and stiff—sister from her marathon kneeling experience.

"Merci, Soeur," she sleepily acknowledged before groggily pulling herself up off her knees and crawling back on to the sofa that temporarily served as her bed. Watching this all-too-familiar preliminary battle with jet lag-enhanced fatigue brought a twinge of envy to my heart as I realized that this sleepy sister was just embarking on her glorious missionary experience when I was far too close to the moment where I would be stepping on a plane to fly home and end it. I wanted somehow to grab the quickly passing hands of time and slow them down just a bit so that I could make these final, never-to-be-forgotten chapters of my missionary experience last just a little bit longer. But for the moment, I knew it was time to focus on the task at hand and help a struggling-to-adjust slumbering sister off of her aching knees—again—and deposit her into the safety of her bed—an act which was quickly becoming my nocturnal routine.

Responding to my light tap on her shoulder as well as the sound of her repeatedly whispered name, the sleeping sister sheepishly raised her head, rubbed her eyes and then with a dramatic sigh that expressed her frustration at having fallen asleep again in the middle of her prayer, she woefully lamented, "I'm sure Heavenly Father is getting a little tired of hearing heavy breathing from me every night!"

"It'll get better, I promise," I assured her as I affectionately patted her on the shoulder and rose from the chair where I had been sitting next to the couch.

"Really? Just when will I stop feeling so tired?" she pleadingly questioned from her pillow.

"In about sixteen months," I playfully responded as I started to turn towards the room where my empty bed waited for my return.

Another sigh issued forth, which was followed by a question that stopped my forward progress. "Soeur," she whispered in a voice that was slightly more awake now than it had been a second ago. "I know it's late, but could you tell me what I can do to help me love my mission as much as I know that you do?" she sincerely requested.

It was a question I hadn't expected, especially at two in the morning, but one that gave me great pause as I turned back towards her and took my place once again in the chair next to the sofa.

In the few moments that followed her request, I wondered what I could possibly say that could let her see how much this mission experience had come to mean to me. I questioned if there could be any way that I could describe how much I had grown, or words I could say that would express how much I had learned about my Savior and about myself. Was it even possible to describe all of the miracles I had seen and answered prayers I had witnessed both in the lives of those I had taught and in my own life?

I wasn't sure where to even begin to express how deeply rooted my testimony and love for the Book of Mormon had become, or how powerful a witness I had received of the prophet Joseph Smith. What could I say that could possibly help her see how deeply I had come to know that my Heavenly Father really knew me and loved me? Or to describe how powerfully I had come to trust in the voice of the Spirit? Would she be able to understand how profoundly I had learned that wherever I went in life, I knew I would never be truly alone?

I was sure there was absolutely no way I could adequately explain the

The Price

hope I had received by witnessing how completely the power of the atonement had changed the lives of those I had taught, and how it had changed mine. I wondered if I could explain how the mountains I had climbed as well as the valleys I had endured had taught me things about myself and about life that I never could have learned otherwise. How could I pass on the invaluable lessons I had learned from discovering that I could push myself harder than I ever knew I was capable of pushing, and that I could love more deeply than I ever knew I was capable of loving?

I wanted to tell her to learn to laugh, and to splash in the rain, and to hold tight to the handle bars when she went over railroad tracks. I wanted to assure her to believe that God could teach her anything she needed to know. I wanted to encourage her to be bold and to trust what the Spirit was telling her to do and to not to worry about or fear the future, but to have faith that the Lord would take care of everything.

I wanted to let her know just how profoundly I had received the answer to my question, thrown to the wind as I pedaled to church that first Sunday nearly a year and a half ago as a young, sweaty and discouraged missionary who wanted to know "What on earth am I doing here?" I wanted her to know that I knew without a doubt what on earth I was doing here, as well as what every other child of God who was ever born on earth was doing here. I wanted to tell her everything that I had learned from this sweet missionary experience. But I didn't. Instead I just told her, "Soeur, give your heart to the Savior, all of it. And love the people." I knew she would learn the rest.

Quietly, I turned out the light, making sure that the now close-to-slumbering sister was safely tucked into her bed, and headed reflectively back to mine.

Sister Felt
Chicago Illinois Mission
(Spanish Speaking) 2013

Post Script

The call to serve the sisters in my ward as Relief Society President had come unexpectedly and during one of the busiest weeks of my teaching job. By the end of each work day—which somehow always seemed to extend itself far beyond the time I was required to be at school no matter how hard I worked—I often found myself completely exhausted and wondering how I was ever going to find the time or the energy to accomplish all that was required of me. The thought of adding to all of that the additional responsibilities of leading my Relief Society frankly overwhelmed me. Although I had made it a matter of personal commitment to always accept a calling to serve in the church, I felt physically and mentally incapable of figuring out how to do all that I knew would be required of me.

After much fasting and prayer, I took my concerns with me to the temple. As I sat reflectively pondering on my new call to serve, a calming voice impressed itself upon my spirit, bringing to mind the very counsel I had given a sleepy missionary many years previously.

"Just give me your heart," it whispered to me, "all of it, and love the sisters. I will help you with you the rest."

I left the temple and drove back home that night feeling quietly reassured that I would be able to do my calling, and that He would teach me how.

"Come unto me, all ye that labour and are heavy laden, and I will give you rest. Take my yoke upon you and learn of me; for I am meek and lowly in heart; and ye shall find rest unto your souls. For my yoke is easy, and my burden is light"
Matthew 11:28.

The Price

CHAPTER TWENTY
Le Cercle

The Circle

It was like giving away an old friend. I could hardly bring myself to do it, but knew that I had to. I had tried to think of every imaginable way that I could take it home with me—and justify the expense—but I knew in my heart, it had to stay. It had served me well over the sixteen months we had been together—that five speed blue and silver bike "et moi"—but it was time for me to go while it still had places to go and things to do.

We had shared so much together and I had learned so very much atop its wide, tan saddle-stitched seat. Enough to last a lifetime—and beyond. Not only had my legs grown stronger and stronger over the past year and a half as we sped about France and Belgium, but so had my testimony—pedal by pedal —during countless reflective rides through beautiful canalled streets and flowered villages.

"Mon vélo" had heard some of the most heartfelt prayers I had ever uttered, both silent and offered in the wind as it whispered past my ears. It had endured endless kilometers of silly road songs and hymns of gratitude from a heart that was perpetually full to bursting. It had carried me dutifully past preliminary days of homesickness and never ending fatigue, delivering me into days of immeasurable joy and thanksgiving. It had splashed me through deluge after deluge of cold coastal rains and picked its way over lightly snow-dusted streets. It had hauled weeks and weeks' worth of laundry and smelly French cheese on its back, and transported converters and projectors on its fenders from one end of the cities I had served in to the other. It had delivered me to the homes of sinners and of priests, and had waited patiently outside countless apartment buildings and humble homes while my companions and I expounded the truths of the gospel to all who would hear. It had revealed to me the beauties of France and Belgium, and had taken me to castles and oceans, down hills and over mountains—to places I had never imagined I would ever go.

With an unexpected lump in my throat, I unstrapped the two light blue saddlebags from off the back fender—souvenirs I had lovingly inherited from one of my returning-home companions—and then guided the handlebars of my bike into the hands of the sister missionary who was to be its new owner.

"Please be good to mon vélo," I said, patting its silver fender. Then I turned and walked away, carrying with me the knowledge that I would never be the same.

Post Script

Fondly, a warm smile crept across my face as I watched the downloaded picture open up on my computer screen. It was immediately evident from the straggly hair that peeked errantly out from under the tipped bike helmet of my former student as well as her somewhat rumpled attire, along with the straggly, rumpled look of the other three sister missionaries who stood holding their bikes beside her in the picture, that the ride they had just finished had been a long and sweaty one. It had been a little over a year since I had sat with her and her two sisters in my classroom while they had excitedly and nervously discussed their upcoming mission plans.

I could easily empathize with the bone-deep fatigue I could detect in those valiant peddlers as they propped themselves up against the handlebars of their bikes. Yet, at the same time, it was impossible to miss the light in their eyes, and the profound sense of joy that etched itself across their faces in the form of four tired but beaming smiles. It was a picture of pure contentment, of an at-oneness with self and with God that comes from being totally and completely worn out in His service. It was a picture I'm sure has repeated itself over and over again through all the years—since sisters have been called to serve missions—like the ever turning wheels of the bikes they'd somehow managed to learn how to ride in a dress.

"Wherefore, the course of the Lord is one eternal round" 1 Nephi 10:19

The Circle

EPILOGUE
Les Notes du Champ

Notes from the Field

"When President Monson announced the age change for serving missions and stated that 'young women are not under the same obligation to serve missions as young men,' I took that to mean that the Lord didn't care whether or not I served a mission—that it was simply a matter of personal preference. As a result, I decided that I had other important things I wanted to do and that a mission wasn't for me. However, there came a point when I realized that I needed to know what the Lord wanted me to do, not just what I wanted to do. Through this experience, I have come to know that the Lord has a personal plan for each of us and what we do in life really does matter to Him. Even though you, as sisters, may not have the same obligation to serve missions as young men do, it is important to make the Lord a part of your decision as to whether or not it is His desire for you to serve a mission. He will give you the right answer—one that is specific for you."

—*Sister Rachel Howard, California Anaheim Mission (Spanish Speaking)*

"I had never, in my entire life, been so tested as I had been preparing to leave on a mission. There were many times I just wanted to give up, but I knew I couldn't. I knew I had been called by God to serve a mission at this time in my life and that there were people only I could reach. I truly believe that I knew people, by name, in the premortal existence and that I loved them. I wanted to do my part to help as many of those people as possible gain exaltation. This is what kept me going."

—*Sister Emily Allen, New Hampshire Manchester Mission*

"I received the answer that I was supposed go on a mission after I had spent a summer reading my scriptures, going to the temple, and praying about whether I should go. The answer came to me while I was reading my patriarchal blessing. Initially, I was scared, wondering if I could leave my family or live in an unfamiliar place. The scripture in Galatians 5:22 that proclaims, 'The fruit of the Spirit is love, joy, peace, longsuffering, gentleness, goodness, faith,' helped me understand the source of my fears. I realized that fear should not have a place in my life. I am serving a mission not only because I love God but also because I have felt His love for me. I want to share this love and help everyone feel the love God has for them."

—*Sister Koelliker, Argentina Resistencia Mission*

"A mission is simply the best and the greatest thing I have ever done. As a missionary, I learned that if I trusted in the Lord and let Him take the reins, He would lead, guide and direct me where I needed to go. Sometimes when I was required to do things that at first were a little hard for me, I found out that if I simply prayed for just 'ten seconds of courage,' that would be enough to help me do what I needed to do."

—*Sister Natalie Bennion, France Paris Mission*

"I knew a mission was going to be hard and wonderful, but I didn't know it was going to be this hard and this wonderful. I have grown up a lot. I have seen a marvelous work come forth not only in the lives of others but in my life as well. I've learned to trust in God's timing, to have faith in the seeds I plant, and to rely on the Spirit to know what to say. I have asked for a lot of things on my mission: strength to get out of bed and put on a smile as well as faith that everything is going to be okay. I've prayed for miracles and answers. For help with investigators and companions. For the safety of myself and my family. For peace. All of my prayers have been answered. God is good."

—*Sister Emma Jackson, South Carolina Columbia Mission*

"I love being a missionary and sharing the gospel with others. The gospel changes people: how they look, act, speak, think—everything! It is only through change and repentance that we are able to submit our will to the Father and become more like Christ."

—*Susanna Ungricht, Washington Spokane Mission*

"I am grateful to be a missionary. It allows me to see my weaknesses more than ever before but also gives me the tools needed to make them strong through the Lord. Sometimes missions are hard, but they are the best kind of hard. There is no greater feeling than coming home every single day completely exhausted, knowing I have given my all to the Lord. Although I still fall short in some areas, through Him I can become strong and try again the next day. I am so grateful for this opportunity to serve in the land of Korea! It's not always easy—no one ever told me it would be—but it is definitely is worth it!"

—*Sister Eliza Glauser, Korea Seoul South Mission*

"This mission experience has opened my eyes to everything I want to do, everything I need to work on, everything I need to become. My mission has lit a passion in me. It has helped me understand how important this work is—it is so much bigger than we are. It has been a complete honor and privilege to serve God in beautiful Thailand. I love these people. I love this land."

—*Sister Grace Jackson, Thailand Bangkok Mission*

"There was a time in my life that I knew what it was like to have the gospel and not to live it. But now that I'm living the gospel—and sharing it with others—I'm the happiest I've ever been. I find so much joy in sharing the gospel. It is so precious to me. When the work is tiring, I think of my Savior. I think of when He was suffering and in pain. He never gave up and He never will give up—on me or on anyone else. So I will never give up. Serving an 18-month mission is just a small token of what He's done for me. It is such an honor to wear His name over my heart as one of His missionaries."

—*Sister Noamaleniu Sydall, Utah Salt Lake City West Mission*

"I will never forget the miracles I saw as I served as a missionary on the island of São Miguel. I learned through my experiences that our Heavenly Father has great things for us to accomplish and will help us do His work."

—*Sister Moriah Fuller, Portugal Lisbon Mission*

Epilogue

"I can't imagine my life if I hadn't made the choice to serve a mission! I have gained so many blessings—both physical and spiritual. One of the most beautiful things I have experienced as a missionary is being able to see a change of heart in the lives of others and in myself. I have learned that the Lord will wait patiently for us to humble ourselves and to make those changes that are necessary to follow Him. I have never accomplished a greater work in my life than serving a mission."

—*Sister Rena Heimuli, Utah Salt Lake City West Mission*

"Words cannot even begin to express the light and understanding that I have gained over these past months. I have never been so physically exhausted but so incredibly happy at the same time. What a strange feeling it is to watch brand new missionaries arrive and begin their journey! What I would give to be them! They have no idea what experiences await them and the joy that they will feel over the next eighteen to twenty-four months. Who knew that I would find such joy sitting in a stranger's home testifying of Christ and of His gospel? This is where true happiness is found. I feel privileged to be a part of such an incredible force for good. What a joy it is to be in the service of our God!" —*Sister Eliza Jackson, Texas San Antonio Mission*

"One of the greatest experiences I had as a missionary was having the Holy Ghost continually touch my heart and manifest to me, and to those I taught, that God lives and that Jesus is the Christ and Savior of the world. Through the Holy Ghost, I was able to know that I was teaching the true restored gospel of Jesus Christ. By this same powerful witness of the Spirit, I was also comforted in the knowledge that Christ is aware of who we are and loves every one of us. This knowledge has sustained me when things that I sometimes don't quite understand happen in my life and in the lives of others. At such times, that overwhelming love of the Lord that I came to know so well on my mission comforts me and brings me peace."

—*Sister Susan Young, California Oakland Mission*

"At the end of my mission, my wonderful mission president didn't give the typical 'go home and get married' advice. Acknowledging that people could not control when they would meet their eternal companions, he counseled us instead to remain faithful to the gospel, keep our covenants, and get an education, emphasizing that when the time was right, we would receive the blessing of eternal marriage. He taught us that all things happen on the Lord's time and that it is our duty to remain worthy to receive the promised blessings so that we will be ready for that time. This was truly the best advice that he could have given me, and this has helped me a lot since my mission. Many people are often amazed at the confidence that I maintain as a single sister in my late 30's in a family-based church. It is because my mission president taught me that all promised blessings will be given in the Lord's own time if I keep my covenants. I know that He knows what is best for each of us. If we will 'wait upon the Lord,' life—and eternity, for that matter—will be much sweeter."

—*Sister Sarah Atherton, West Virginia Charleston Mission*

"After forty years of marriage and raising eight children together, my husband and I thought we knew each other completely, but we have grown so much closer through the months we've served together as senior missionaries. What a wonderful blessing this has been! I've seen firsthand how much senior couples and senior sister missionaries are needed. I've learned that the most important thing sisters can share with the members, besides their testimonies, is their love. Many of the members in Rwanda suffered through the dark days of the genocide against the Tutsi. They have embraced the restored gospel of Jesus Christ and have a deep love of their Savior because they know He was with them during those terrifying days. The phrase 'families are forever' takes on a special meaning in Rwanda. I'll always be thankful that I was blessed with the opportunity to serve a mission here with my husband."

—*Sister Kathryn Palmer, Uganda Kampala Mission*

Epilogue

APPENDIX
Pardon My French

*An alphabetized glossary of French terms
that appear in this book*

À la mode: in style

À mon chevet: at my bedside

Adieu: farewell (literally: at God)

Arrêt: a stop

Au revoir: good-bye

Bateau: boat

Bien fait: well done

Bien: well

Bienvenue: welcome

Bise: kiss on either cheek

**Bonjour Hélène. Bonjour Paul.
Ça va? Oui, ça va et toi?:**
Hello Helen. Hello Paul. How are you?

Bonjour mes chers frères et sœurs:
Hello my dear brothers and sisters.

Bonjour: hello

Bonjour. Je m'appelle Hélène: Hello, my name is Helen.

Bonne chance: good luck

Boulangerie: bakery

Campagne: countryside

Cartes de Noël: Christmas cards

Chef d'œuvre: Masterpiece

Chemin: path, lane

Cheval: horse

Chevet: bedside

Chez moi: at my home

Comment ça va?: How are you? (familiar)

Comment-allez-vous? How are you? (formal)

D'où venez-vous?: Where are you from?

Dans l'appartement: in the apartment

Déjà-vu: already seen

Dieu soit avec toi: God be with you.

Dis donc, où est la bibliothèque?:
Say, where is the library?

Drôle: funny, droll

En herbe: budding

En plein milieu: right in the middle

En route: in route, on the way

En train: in a train

En ville: downtown

Escargots: snails

Et moi: and me

Facteur: mailman

Fête de Saint Nicolas: Celebration of Saint Nicolas

Feu rouge: red light

Francophone: French speaking

Francs: former unit of money equivalent to about a quarter in U.S. money

Gare: train station

Grand quartier: big neighborhood or area

Grande salle: big room

Je m'excuse: excuse me

Je ne sais pas: I don't know.

Appendix

Je ne sais quoi: pleasing quality that cannot be described

Kiosque: booth

L'Église de Jésus-Christ Des Saints des Derniers Jours:
The Church of Jesus Christ of Latter-Day Saints

L'instructeur: teacher

L'invitation: the invitation

La campagne: the countryside

La connaissance: knowledge

La destination populaire: the popular destination

La guerre: the war

La parole: the word

La pluie: the rain

La promesse: the promise

La réponse: the answer

La voix: the voice

Le café, le thé ou les boissons alcoolisées:
coffee, tea or alcoholic drinks

Le cantique: the hymnal

Le cercle: the circle

Le compagnon: the companion

Le début: the beginning

Le don: the gift

Le prix: the price

Le voyage: the trip

Les boissons alcoolisées: alcoholic drinks

Les fêtes: the holidays, celebrations

Les frères: the brothers, brethren

Les fruits et noix: fruit and nuts

Les plaques d'or: the gold plates

Les sœurs: the sisters

Les soldats: the soldiers

Les toilettes: the restroom

Leur: their

Ma petite grand-mère: my little grandmother
("petite" is often used as an endearment)

Mal du pays: homesickness

Mannequin: model

Merci: Thank you.

Merci, Soeur: Thank you, Sister.

Mes anges: my angels

Mon vélo: my bike

Non merci: No thank you.

Non: no

Non, Ce n'est pas comme ça!:
No, it's not like that! That's not right!

Oui!: yes

Oui, c'est ça: Yes, that's it.

Petite salle: little room

Petite boisson: little drink

Petite grand-mère: little grandmother
("petite" is used as an endearment)

Petite victoire: small victory

Plat: a platter or dish

Politesse: politeness

Porte à Porte: tracting

Quartier: neighborhood or area

Qui que ce soit: whoever it is

Rendez-vous: an appointment or meeting

Réveillon: a big meal generally held on
Christmas or New Year's Eve

Appendix

Rez-de-chaussée: ground floor

Sale: dirty

Salle: room

Sans: without

Sapin: fir tree, notably a Christmas tree

Savoir faire: know how

Soeurs Missionnaires: Sister Missionaries

Son amour: His love

Terre: the earth, dirt

Tour de France: Tour of France

Trop dangereux: too dangerous

Trottoir: sidewalk

Un petit morceau de pain: a little piece of bread

Une grosse tête: knowledgeable (literally: a big head)

Une petite soirée: a little evening get together

Venir: to come

Viennent: third person conjugation of "to come" as in "they come"

Vous américains!: You Americans!

Vous n'êtes pas d'ici: You are not from here.

Sources

"What Is My Purpose as a Missionary?" *Preach My Gospel: A Guide to Missionary Service,* Salt Lake City: The Church of Jesus Christ of Latter-Day Saints, 2004. 1–16.

Ballard, M. Russell. "What Matters Most Is What Lasts Longest," October 2005 General Conference Report.

Ballard, M. Russell. "Is it Worth it?" Brigham Young University Fireside, 2 Sept. 1979.

Bednar, David A. "The Tender Mercies of the Lord," April 2005 General Conference Report.

Cook, Gene R. "Moroni's Promise," *Ensign* April 1994.

Eyring, Henry B. "Rise to Your Call," October 2002 General Conference Report.

Eyring, Henry B. "How Great Shall Be Your Joy," *Liahona* Feb. 2011.

Eyring, Henry B. "Mountains to Climb," *Ensign* May 2012.

Hales, Robert D. "Gifts of the Spirit," *Ensign* Feb. 2002.

Holland, Jeffery R. "The Atonement," New Mission President Seminar, Provo MTC, 2007.

Holland, Jeffery R. "The Miracle of a Mission," Brazil CTM, 28 Oct. 2000.

Kimball, Spencer W. "Tragedy or Destiny," Brigham Young University Speeches of the Year, 6 December 1955: 6.

Milner, Nita Dale. "When I am Baptized," *Primary Children's Hymn Book.* 1989. 103.

President Thomas S. Monson, "We Never Walk Alone," *Ensign* Oct. 2013.

Oaks, Dallin H. "Teaching and Learning by the Spirit," *Liahona* May 1999.

Richardson, Matthew O, "Teaching after the Manner of the Spirit," *Ensign* Oct. 2011.

Scott, Richard G. "To Acquire Spiritual Guidance," *Ensign* Nov. 2009.

Smith, Joseph F. Doctrines of Salvation. 3 vols. 1954-56. 1:47–48.

Uchtdorf, Dieter F. "Continue in Patience," *Ensign* April 2010.

Images courtesy iStock/Thinkstock.com, *pages xiv, 146, 150*

Sources